The Gift of Human Sexuality

The Gift of Human Sexuality

A Christian Perspective

- A Handbook for Parents and Teens -

EDUARDO M. AZCARATE, Ph.D.

Youth Apostles Institute McLean, Virginia

Youth Apostles Institute
1600 Carlin Ln.
McLean, VA 22101
(703) 556-0914
http://www.youthapostles.org/

Printed in the United States of America
ISBN: 0-974-3358-0-0

I dedicate this book to my parents, my wife Ana, my children Eddy, AnaMari, Elena, and MariTere, and their spouses. I especially dedicate it to my grandchildren. It is my prayer that they grow into holy, whole, and healthy men and women.

I am most thankful to the many friends and relatives who have helped me in the production of this manuscript. I am also grateful to the many young people who, through their trust and openness, have challenged me to reflect on God's most beautiful gift of human sexuality.

Table of Contents

Illustrations

Acknowledgments: The illustrations in this book were prepared by Dr. Azcarate. Figures 1-12 and 14 are modeled on illustrations found in Parent and Child Institute, *The Life Cycle Library* (Chicago: Parent and Child Institute, 1969). Figure 15 is modeled on an illustration that originally appeared in C. Dienhart, *Basic Human Anatomy and Physiology* (Philadelphia: Saunders, 1967).

Introduction

A Word to Parents

Parents often ask me what they should read in order to effectively teach their children about human sexuality. They express their belief in the need to educate their kids and their willingness to do it. However, they feel unsure about what and how much to say regarding human development and Christian sexual values.

I have taught the Christian values underlying God's great gift of sexuality to young people between fifth grade and twelfth grade for more than twenty-five years. For much of that time I recommended sources to read, but was prompted by parents to write my own book on the subject. I decided to accept the challenge.

The book begins with a reflection on who God is and what sexuality is. It describes the miracle of life in the womb, the value of all life, abortion, and adoption. It moves on to a description of fundamental changes of puberty and the transcendental nature of the act of sexual love. It describes secondary sexual characteristics of boys and girls. It covers issues of privacy and curiosity and leads into an understanding of the virtue of chastity. It discusses the value of relationships in adolescence and the importance of pre-marital chastity. It talks about homosexuality, family planning, sexually transmitted diseases, and other sexual issues and disorders. It ends with a challenge to young people to recognize that each person is called to be holy.

I wrote this book for you to read together with your child, aloud if possible. Ideally, both parents will read it with one child at a time. If only one parent can do it, the gender of the parent does not matter.

After some sections, there is a box for discussion. The more openness and communication that exists between parents and their children, the better are their children's chances at a healthy sexual development. Once you have finished reading this book, you may also wish to review my booklet *Healthy Sexual Development—The Key to Chastity.*

A parent, or other adult approved by the parents, is primarily responsible to form the Christian conscience of his or her child. I have written the book with the needs and learning level of junior high students in mind, but I hope you will read through the book on your own before beginning it with your child. You should then decide the time at which you think it is best to share this information with your son or daughter. It is my hope that you will read the book in sections over several days or weeks. You may find it worth re-reading some sections, depending on the level of your child's understanding, the questions the reading generates, and the amount of open discussion it produces. I recommend the entire book for junior high students, but you must rely on your wisdom and judge according to your child's knowledge and maturity when determining what to read with your children.

The first eight chapters could be easily understood by fifth and sixth graders with some parental help. Children who are not yet into puberty are less resistant to studying this type of material. Chapter 10, on the virtue of chastity, can be read early on but might not be fully understood without the material covered in Chapter 9. Chapters 11 through 17 could be read in junior high but should be revisited during high school.

Christian formation can only take place by properly informing young people about all areas of human sexuality. Hesitant parents need to keep in mind that children endure excessive exposure to sexual matters in today's society. It is reasonable to assume that by age eleven or twelve, and sometimes long before that, a young person has been exposed to sexual issues. Even if a particular child is not exposed to mixed messages or undesirable sexual material, the risk is always present. It is better to prepare young people for what they may see, hear, or read regarding sexuality than to deny the risk, avoid the issues, and fail to properly form the child's conscience.

Some subjects covered in this book could make some parents uncomfortable. The uneasy feeling may not be related to the age or maturity of their son or daughter, but to the state of things in the society in which we live.

Children and teens are exposed, through the media and their peers, to all kinds of confusing and offensive material. I hope you understand that by the time the contents of this book are shared and discussed, your children may already have some awareness of the issues I present here.

Please keep in mind that this book responds to thousands of questions that ten- to fifteen-year-old boys and girls have asked me over the years. I agonized over whether to include certain delicate issues. I finally decided to follow my conviction that adequate knowledge is the best route to goodness and inner peace. I strongly believe that it is best to have parents or other responsible adults be the first ones to cover every sexual question and doubt.

1

The Marvelous Gift of Sexuality

Who Is God?

God has been described in many ways, but for the purpose of this book let us simply state that God is a loving creator. Yes, God is the giver of **life** who made *you* out of **love**! Whether you are studying the furthest stars and galaxies or the tiniest microscopic cells, you are always probing God's creation. When studying the human person, God's most marvelous creation, you realize more fully his majesty. Such amazement makes human beings ask God:

> What is man that you should be mindful of him... [yet] you have made him little less than the angels, and crowned him with glory and honor. (Ps 8:5-6)

God has created the entire universe and all that is in it out of love for you. Only humans can study God's creation and love him back for all that he has made. You are his unique creation. You are his special love. Each person is cast in God's image.

> In your wisdom [you] have established man ... to govern the world in holiness and justice. (Wis 9:2-3)

Wait a minute, you may ask, is this a religion book or a book about human sexuality? The answer is "yes!" The two are inseparable.

What Is Sexuality?

Sexuality is the power God has given you to create life and to give and receive love. He who is the Source of All Life has invited you to help him in his task of creation. He who is Love gave you a spiritual soul that enables you to think, choose, and act freely, and to love in a special human way. He also gave you a physical body with unique possibilities, and blessed your body with a specific male or female **gender**. The body of a man and a woman have different sexual organs or **genitals** that together are capable of producing new life. God made it so; people did not invent this arrangement.

> God created man in His image: in the divine image He created him; male and female He created them. (Gen 1:27)

He created each human being as a sexual person, and what he creates is good and beautiful.

It is amazing to realize that the essence of both God and human sexuality is **life** and **love**. This very important gift—to love and to transmit life—has to be taken very seriously. Sexuality is an amazing and delicate gift, and like any special gift it has to be protected carefully. If you are given a very expensive watch or ring that has been passed down to you through the generations, you would not play around with it carelessly, and you would most probably wear it only on special occasions.

How can the gift of genital sexuality be best protected? By reserving genital sexual love for marriage. The **sacrament of Matrimony** blesses the union of a man and a woman who then become spouses. The two spouses make a **commitment** to God and promise to love one another, to form a family, and to create and protect human life. Genital sexual love is reserved for committed spouses.

Unfortunately, the gift of sexuality is sometimes not taken seriously by some people who refer to sex with inaccurate, slangy, disrespectful, or vulgar language. They treat sex cheaply; they think it is like a toy watch in a cereal box rather than the complex and expensive watch that it is. You will hear stories in which life is disrespected, or even coldly discarded. You may also hear stories or witness times when sex has nothing to do with love. Children are exposed to sexual stories, pornographic materials like magazines or movies, or even traumatic personal experiences. These children and teens often grow up thinking about human sexuality as something dirty. Sexuality is not dirty, it is God's gift to us. You need to learn about this gift and have the freedom to talk about sexuality with your parents or other adults whom you and your parents trust.

Talking about sex can be embarrassing. I hope this book will ease your mind. When you were born, your parents made a commitment to help you grow and to provide for your education. They made you out of love and took care of all your needs. They fed you, bathed you, and made sure that every part of your body, including your sexual organs, was healthy and clean. They know you well, and if you are too embarrassed, perhaps that is so because you have heard too many bad things about sex from other people. It is much better to learn important and complex issues like human sexuality from your parents than from anyone else. This book is a good opportunity to get you and your parents to sit down and discuss it together. Give yourself a chance to learn about sexuality with them.

Please keep in mind that although some sexual stories, events, or experiences may be bad, God's creation of sexuality is still always good and beautiful. Think about another one of God's gifts: fire. Fire can make you warm, and help you cook or melt metals with which to make useful objects. But you are not supposed to play with fire because it can also burn you and leave you with scars, or destroy your house and the things you treasure. God's creation of fire is fantastic but we human beings may misuse it and harm ourselves and others. The same is true of human sexuality. It is God's beautiful gift of life and love, but human beings sometimes abuse or misuse it.

2

Growing Up Inside Your Mother

Life in the Womb

Your life began inside your mother. For about nine months you lived in your mother's **womb**, before you were even seen or held by your parents. Her womb, or **uterus**, is a special place that her body used exclusively during pregnancy to hold you and help you develop. Before the pregnancy, her uterus resembled the shape and size of an upside-down pear. When your mother became pregnant, it began to expand to allow space for you as you grew. Some children think unborn babies are inside their mothers' "bellies." It is important to note that you were not inside your mother's stomach, but inside her uterus.

At the first moment of your **conception**, you were a single cell, no bigger than the tip of a pin. It was then that your life began; the moment in which you were conceived was the instant in which God blessed you with an immortal soul. From the moment you began to exist inside your mother's womb, you were constantly growing and developing. Within two weeks, your brain began to form and you were thousands of cells big. In about twenty-five days, your heart was beating and your arms and legs were beginning to develop. (For a summary of a baby's development inside its mother, please turn the page and study Figure 1.)

As your body grew inside your mother, her uterus continued to expand and you developed an **umbilical cord**. The umbilical cord is a long and thick cord that connects the baby to the **placenta**. It allows the mother's blood to pass to the baby, bringing oxygen and food and taking away waste matters. It varies in size from seven inches to four feet. Your **navel**, "belly button," or **umbilicus**, serves as a reminder that you were once connected to your mother's placenta.

The **placenta**, which develops on the wall of the uterus, is like a relay station that supervises the blood supply that comes from the mother's body to feed the baby through the umbilical cord. In Figure 2, you can see the umbilical cord and the placenta. The blood returns to the placenta through the umbilical

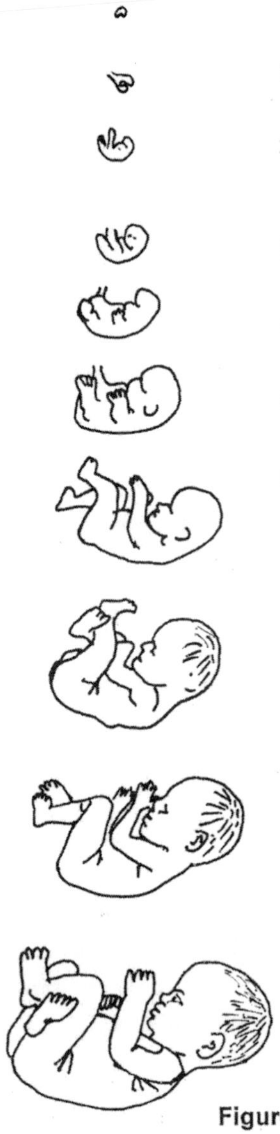

Age	Development	Size
1 day	Fertilized egg cell. No bigger than a dot.	
15 days	Thousands of cells. Brain forming.	
25 days	Heart beating. Beginning of arms and legs.	Length: ± 1 inch
35 days	Eyes, ears, and skeleton forming.	
45 days	Outline of fingers. Toes formed.	Length: ± 2 in.
60 days	Baby begins to move.	
95 days	Most body systems are now working.	Length: ± 3 in. Weight: ± 1 oz.
125 days	Skin and hair. Baby can be seen as human. Mother feels the baby.	Length: ± 4 in.
200 days	Baby almost ready. Needs to gain weight and strength.	Length: ± 8 in. Weight: ± 5 lbs.
266 days	Birth occurs. Breathing and digestion begin.	Length: ± 16 in. Weight: ± 7 lbs.

Figure 1 - Stages of Fetal Development

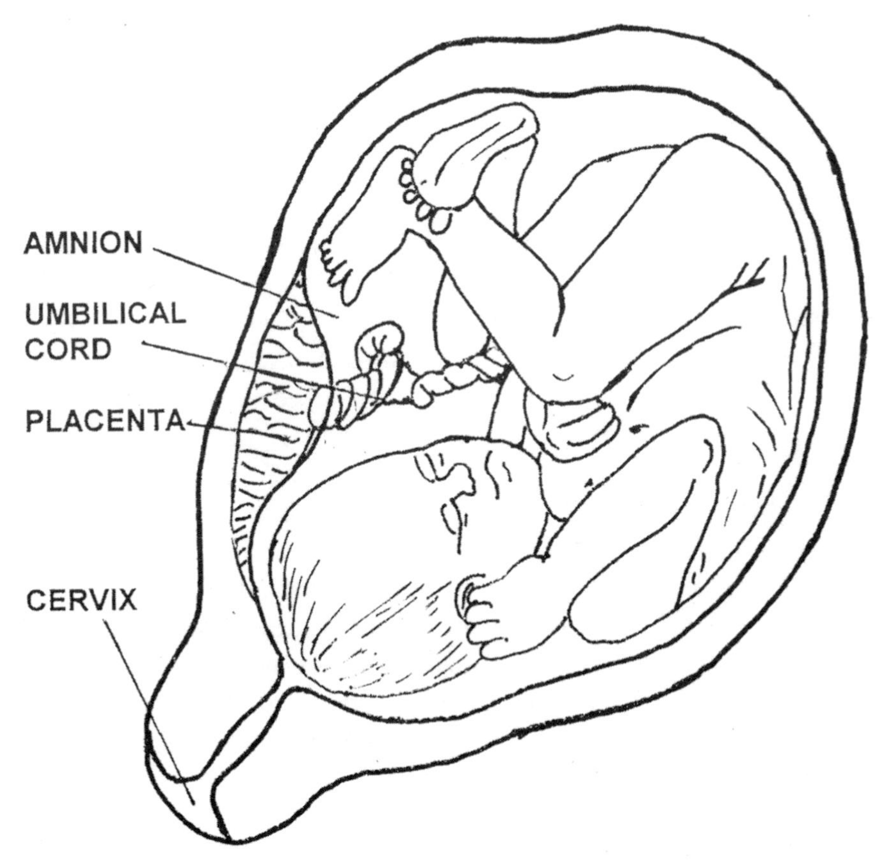

Figure 2
Six Month-old Baby in Uterus

cord after providing the baby with the necessary nutrients. From the placenta, the blood then goes back into the mother's blood stream, picks up the supply of food it needs, and returns to the placenta.

During the nine months inside the mother, the baby lives inside a **sac** called the **amnion**. The baby floats inside the amniotic sac in a fluid called **amniotic fluid**. This amniotic fluid protects the baby inside the uterus during the mother's pregnancy. It is important to stress that inside a mother's womb babies do not breathe regularly or eat through their mouth. Sometimes, though, they may breathe in or swallow some of the amniotic fluid. As already mentioned, babies are kept alive through the blood, rich in oxygen and nutrients, that the mother passes on through the placenta and the umbilical cord. (Some children think blood is repulsive, but blood is actually what keeps a person alive.) After the oxygenated blood passes through the baby's body, it returns back to the mother through the cord and the placenta.

In about three months, most body systems are working and the doctor can already tell if the baby is going to be a boy or a girl. The baby then weighs less than one ounce and is already a sexual being. The **fetus**, as a baby is called inside the mother, still needs to develop skin and hair, and gain enough weight and strength to be able to live on its own outside the mother's uterus. After nine months inside the mother, the baby is ready to be born.

The Process of Birth

If everything goes according to plan at the time of the birth, or **delivery**, of the baby, the baby's head should point downward inside the uterus as it appears in Figure 2. The birth is made possible because the mother's body begins to experience **contractions.** With each **contraction** the uterus tightens, and, after a few seconds, softens. Contractions help the baby go down the birth canal. But there is even more to it than that.

- The **cervix** thins out and then expands, or **dilates**;
- the bone structure in the mother's lower back expands;
- the **amniotic sac** the baby was in while inside the mother breaks open; and,
- sometimes the shape of the baby's head changes to facilitate delivery.

In other words, the contractions help the cervix, which is at the lower end of the uterus, become thin and begin to dilate. The contractions also facilitate a slight loosening of the mother's lower back bones. With each contraction the cervix and birth canal open up more and more and help the baby move down the birth canal. Contractions occur many times over several hours, or even days. At the time of the birth, the amnion breaks open and the amniotic fluid is released.

The head is the largest structure in a baby's body at the time of birth. As a baby goes down the birth canal, the bones in the baby's head sometimes squish a bit upwards. This way the head occupies less space inside the birth canal, and it makes the birth process easier for both the mother and the baby. This is the reason why adults usually remind you to be careful with the head of a newborn baby. The head bones have not yet closed up to protect the baby's brain and the baby needs to be handled with care.

Take a look at Figure 3 and imagine how the baby works his or her way down the mother's **birth canal**, or **vagina**, and out through the entrance of the vagina. The entrance of the vagina is part of the woman's sexual organs. It continues inside the body and connects with the cervix and the uterus.

People sometimes wonder why babies cry when they are born. Babies cry to expand their lungs and to begin to breathe on their own. If babies were not

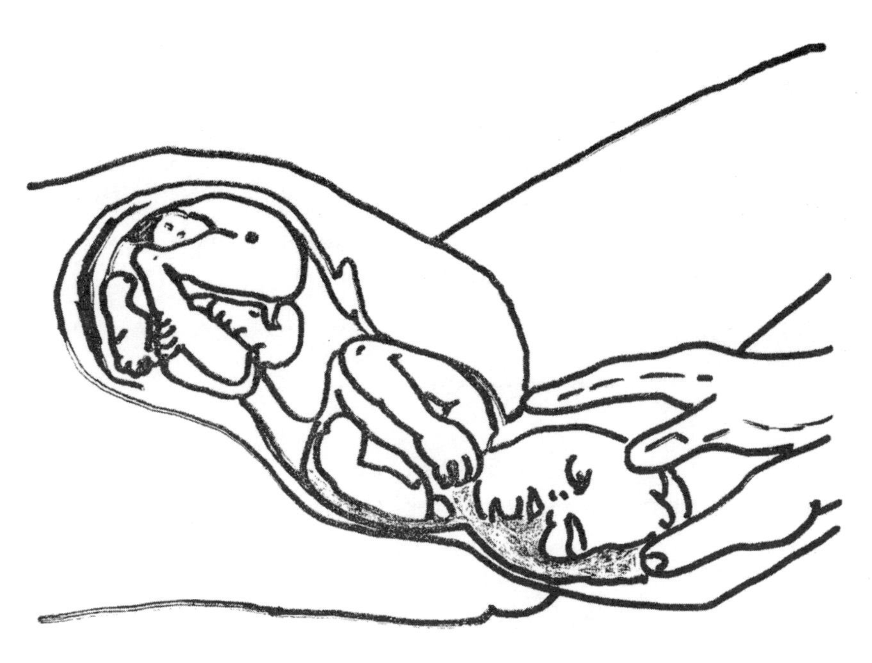

Figure 3
Nine Month-old Baby
About to be Born

able to breathe, they would begin to turn blue, a sign that they lack oxygen. With a flick on the sole of their feet, or a kind but vigorous back-rub, babies may be helped to start breathing on their own. Also, note that only half of the baby's heart functions inside the mother. After babies are born and begin to breathe, their blood picks up oxygen from their lungs. The oxygenated blood then rushes into the half of the heart that was not functioning before, and they finally become capable of living on their own.

After the baby is born the umbilical cord is cut. This hurts neither the mother nor the baby. The cord and the placenta come out of the uterus after the baby is born and become dead skin that is no longer useful. The doctor holds the cord with a clamp and it is cut about one inch away from the baby's body. In about a week, the skin between the baby's body and the place where it was clamped falls off. This process does not hurt the baby or the mother. Once the dried-up, dead skin falls away, the baby has a navel, or belly button.

It is normal to make comparisons and to become curious about your developing body and the bodies of others, including insignificant parts such as belly buttons. A belly button is nothing more than a small scar that reminds you that you were once connected to your mother. Some belly buttons go in deeply, especially as a person grows older, and some stick out a bit forever. "Innies" and "outies" are both normal. It makes no difference which one you have, and belly buttons have nothing to do with sexuality!

To review, the typical way in which the birth takes place can be summarized as follows.

1) The process of birth starts with contractions of the uterus.
2) The baby passes through the cervix.
3) The baby moves down through the birth canal.
4) The baby emerges comes out through the entrance of the mother's vagina.

Sometimes the baby's head is not pointed downwards toward the cervix. Instead, the legs or the rear end point downwards. These **breech positions** can impede vaginal delivery. Other times the doctor knows that the mother's body is too small for the large baby she is holding inside her uterus, or the baby experiences distress during attempted vaginal delivery. In those cases the baby is delivered through a **cesarean section**, or **c-section**, surgery. This is a simple surgery in which the mother is put to sleep, a horizontal surgical cut, or incision, is made through the abdomen and the uterus, and the baby is removed from inside the mother. If this kind of planned c-section takes place, the next baby may still be born through a normal delivery. Sometimes in an emergency, to save the life of the baby or the mother, a vertical incision is made. In that case, the next baby will probably need to be born through a planned c-section.

Take time to reflect with your parents on the beauty and complexity of God's creation. From one cell to millions of cells, from a dot to a fully developed baby, special cells grow to form the brain, the heart, the eyes, the sexual organs. Each finger, each little bone inside your ear, every large and small part of your body is evidence of the miracle that you are. You did not give yourself life. Your parents merely contributed to God's plan for your existence. All life must be respected because it is made by God. We come from God and we go back to God. We never cease to exist. The life of the baby inside the mother must be protected because it is human life with an immortal soul that belongs to God.

3

The Sacred Value of Human Life

A Reflection on Abortion

All life is sacred because it comes from God who is its creator. However, some people are not respectful of life as a gift from God. They fail to understand that life begins at the moment of conception when God gives the new human person a soul. If the pregnancy is dangerous, difficult, or troublesome to the mother, these people believe the mother has the right to end the pregnancy by means of a "therapeutic" abortion. A therapeutic abortion, hereafter referred to simply as **abortion**, is the act of killing the baby who is inside the mother's womb.

Before the fifth or sixth month of a pregnancy, it is very difficult for the baby to live on its own outside the mother's womb. There are examples of this occurring, but it is not usually possible. If the baby is purposefully removed from the mother's womb before he or she is ready to live, the baby will die. Abortion is a sin because it kills human life, created by God at the moment of conception.

God is the giver of all life. In the Old Testament we read:

> Truly you have formed my inmost being; you knit me in my mother's womb. (Ps 139:13)

Also,

> The Lord called me from birth, from my mother's womb he gave me my name. (Is 49:1)

As Christians we do not condemn sinners, only the sin. Every woman who has had an abortion needs our love and our prayers. We may not judge people. Only God can do that, and he is a most loving and forgiving God. However, we must certainly stand against abortion and pray for the end of all abortions.

Some people take a stand against abortion except in cases where the doctors believe the baby is going to be defective or the mother's life is in danger. These people think the life of the mother is more important than the life of the child. But no exceptions should ever be made because all life is sacred and ultimately comes from God. Babies who have a defect should never be destroyed because they are God's loved ones; they can still bring great joy and consolation to the family. If a pregnancy threatens the mother's health, we must remember that medical doctors are trained to make every effort to save the life of the mother *and* the baby. If, in the process of trying to save both, one of them dies, that is profoundly sad but not morally wrong. There is no fault on the part of the doctor if every effort was made to preserve both lives. Most of the time it is difficult to predict whether the life of the mother or the baby is in the greater danger.

Abortions vs. Miscarriages

Sometimes the life inside the womb dies on its own. This is called a **miscarriage**, or spontaneous abortion. A miscarriage should not be confused with a *therapeutic* abortion because it is not done on purpose. Natural death is different from murder.

Miscarriages happen for different reasons. Sometimes the uterus cannot support the baby's life because there is something medically wrong with the mother. Sometimes the baby itself is defective and cannot live inside the mother. Sometimes the baby dies toward the end of the pregnancy because of a malfunction of the baby's body. When the death occurs at the very end of the pregnancy, it is sometimes called "stillbirth."

Miscarriages are not sinful. Neither the mother nor the doctor are responsible for that sad event. Since babies have an immortal soul from the moment of conception, they live with God eternally should they die from abortions or miscarriages.

A Special Note on Adoption

Sometimes a husband and wife wish to have a family, but are unable to have children because of physical problems that make pregnancy impossible. These spouses wish to be parents and may either apply to an adoption agency or make private arrangements to adopt. The adoption agency studies the situation and matches the couple with a baby or with a woman who is pregnant and cannot keep her baby. Sometimes the woman is too young, has family difficulties or financial problems, or is unable to care for the newborn baby. Women who put a baby up for adoption are very careful to select a good home for the baby and may have many meetings with the agency or person arranging the adoption. In some cases they may even meet the baby's future parents. This decision is made before the baby is born in order to provide well for the baby's future.

Notice I am using the words "mother" and "father" only for the adoptive parents. The baby, although not biologically made by them, is truly theirs. If you are adopted, you are *really* your adopted mother and father's son or daughter. They longed for you and cared for you from the moment you were given to them, usually a few days to a few weeks after your birth. Like every other child, you have only one set of parents. Your face or physique may not look like theirs, but that is true of many children, who may look less like their parents than some distant relative. There is more to human life than physical features. The most important factor in the healthy development of children is the constant love and teaching of their biological or adoptive parents. It really does not make a difference whether you came out from your mother's womb, were given to your parents wrapped in a blanket, or walked into their arms.

If you are not adopted, please do not pity or tease adopted children. They have real parents and a real home just like you. Their parents love them as much as if they were their biological children, and will provide for them in the same fashion. Biological and adoptive parents have the same responsibilities for their children according to the law. Adoption is a real blessing because it provides the adoptive parents and their child the love and security everyone desires and needs. Adoption also protects the life of a baby who otherwise may be aborted, and it gives a couple who is unable to have children the joy of having one of their own. Jesus had an adoptive father who loved him, helped him to grow up, and taught him how to be a carpenter.

Take time to thank your parents for giving you life physically, emotionally, and spiritually. Thank them for taking care of you every day since you were born. Thank God for your parents and pray for them so they can continue to provide adequately for the needs of their family. As you get older you begin to realize that your parents are not perfect. They sometimes lose their temper, worry too much, or become too demanding for your taste. Talk to them about your moods and expectations, but be assured that they love you and wish all the best for you. If they worry, it is because they love you.

Since I hope your parents are reading this book with you, this is a good time for you and them to take a break so they can tell you how awesome and wonderful you are. Parents spend a lot of time correcting and challenging their children; it is part of their job. Parents also need to spend time loving and praising their children. I believe that hugs and kisses are effective in expressing love within the family. They also educate us in human sexuality. I pray that neither parents nor children let a day go by in which there is no expression of affection among all family members.

4

Growing Up from Birth to Puberty

After birth, babies continue on their uninterrupted course of growth. You can go back to your baby pictures and observe your increased height and weight, and other changes that took place through the first few years of your life. You will probably see most of these changes in the first three or four years. After that, the changes are less noticeable until you reach **puberty**. Puberty is another period of accelerated change that happens as children move from girlhood to womanhood, or from boyhood to manhood.

Just before puberty begins, young people often experience an accelerated increase in height and weight. The sexual organs continue to develop, but the changes take place slowly, so children often don't even realize they are happening. During these years there is also an increased capacity for learning and understanding. Boys and girls begin to take more notice of physical differences between men and women. Children going through puberty may also notice their sexual feelings. In addition, some may have learned things about sex when they were younger. Each person is different, has different experiences, and grows within a unique family setting.

Take time to share with your parents the feelings and experiences you have had during childhood. Be reassured that nothing is too embarrassing to share with parents. Trust that they will not be upset with you over this kind of discussion. It is very relieving to share anything that has to do with sexuality, no matter how small or insignificant. If it is difficult to get into a lengthy discussion, you and your parents may want to go on reading. This book may provide answers to some of your questions, or shed light on some situations you may have faced.

Puberty Changes

"Puberty" comes from the Latin word *pubis*, the name of that part of the hipbone that forms the front arch of the pelvis. The **pelvis** is the bone structure that supports the sexual organs, or genitals. Figure 4 shows the **pelvic bone** without the genitals.

Puberty can take place as early as eight or nine years of age and as late as age sixteen. Development does not depend on how old you are (i.e., your chronological age), but on physiological changes, and that is your *developmental* age. Developmental age is related to puberty and puberty finds its beginning with the activity of the **pituitary gland**. The pituitary gland is an organ inside the brain that functions like a master computer chip, which, along with other factors, decides the best time—and the best pace—for your puberty changes to take place. For example, one person may start early, say at age twelve, and achieve adult physical development by age fifteen, which is a fast rate. Another person may start at age twelve and not finish until they turn nineteen—a slow rate. The contrary can also happen: a person may start late and move through puberty at a fast rate; or start late and still move at a slow pace, and keep on growing until age twenty-one or so.

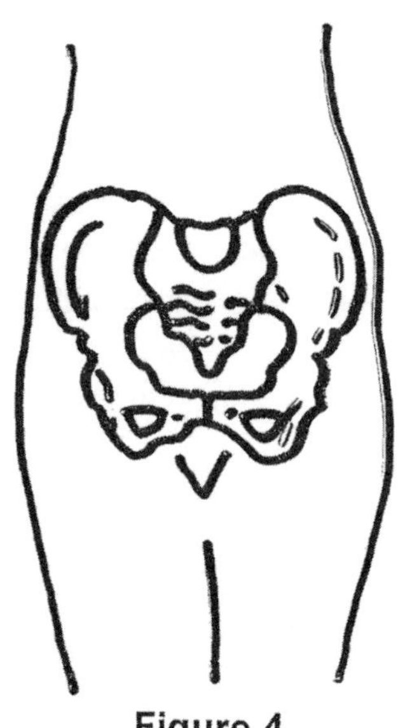

Figure 4
Pelvic Bone

Most teens do not like to be super-early or super-late in their development because they do not want to look too different from their peers. Late growers usually worry more than early ones about their development, and may even wonder if they will grow up at all. The American mentality is that early and fast is better than slow and late. That may be true for running track but it is not true in sexual development. Your body knows the best time for your puberty changes to take place. Whether you like it or not, you may have to accept an early start to your development, or be patient and wait in the case of a delayed puberty. The timing and rate of a young person's development is inherited and varies among families. The age at which your father or mother reached puberty can affect your development. You may want to ask them when they went through puberty.

Above all, be assured that you will grow! If there were any questions about your sexual growth, the doctor would have already mentioned it to you or your parents. I encourage you to be daring and ask your doctor about your sexual development during your next physical examination, even if you do not have any doubts. It is good to hear from a professional that your development is normal, especially if you think you are growing late compared to your peers.

As I mentioned before, puberty changes depend on the activity of the pituitary gland. The pituitary gland is an **endocrine gland**, which means that the gland's hormone travels inside the body by way of the blood vessels. In Figure 5, you can see that the pituitary gland produces a **hormone** that activates the development of the **testicles** (in the case of the male) and the **ovaries** (in the case of the female). These organs produce androgen and estrogen hormones that activate the development of linear growth (height), and of primary and secondary sexual characteristics. The male produces more androgen, the female more estrogen. It is important to keep in mind that, on average, girls grow two years ahead of boys. In other words, if you took into account the development of all the boys and all the girls in the world, the average girl would be ahead of the average boy by two years during puberty.

Keep in mind that you do not want to be in too much of a rush to go through puberty and develop adult sexual characteristics. First you want to grow taller, because that is usually done once all the physiological changes of puberty are finished. In any case, relax, because it is out of your hands. There are no shortcuts or tricks to changing your destined height and physical development. If some insecure kid comments on your early or late development, you might say jokingly, "Talk to my pituitary gland!" When they are insecure, people tend to attack those around them, thinking that their cut downs will give them extra strength or security. Junior high is a particularly stressful time because teens have trouble accepting differences, as if they were contagious. Please avoid cut downs and negative labeling; it harms your peers' emotional development. If you have been the object of this kind of insult, keep in mind that time is in your favor. You will develop physically, and others may grow emotionally and stop resorting to insulting comments.

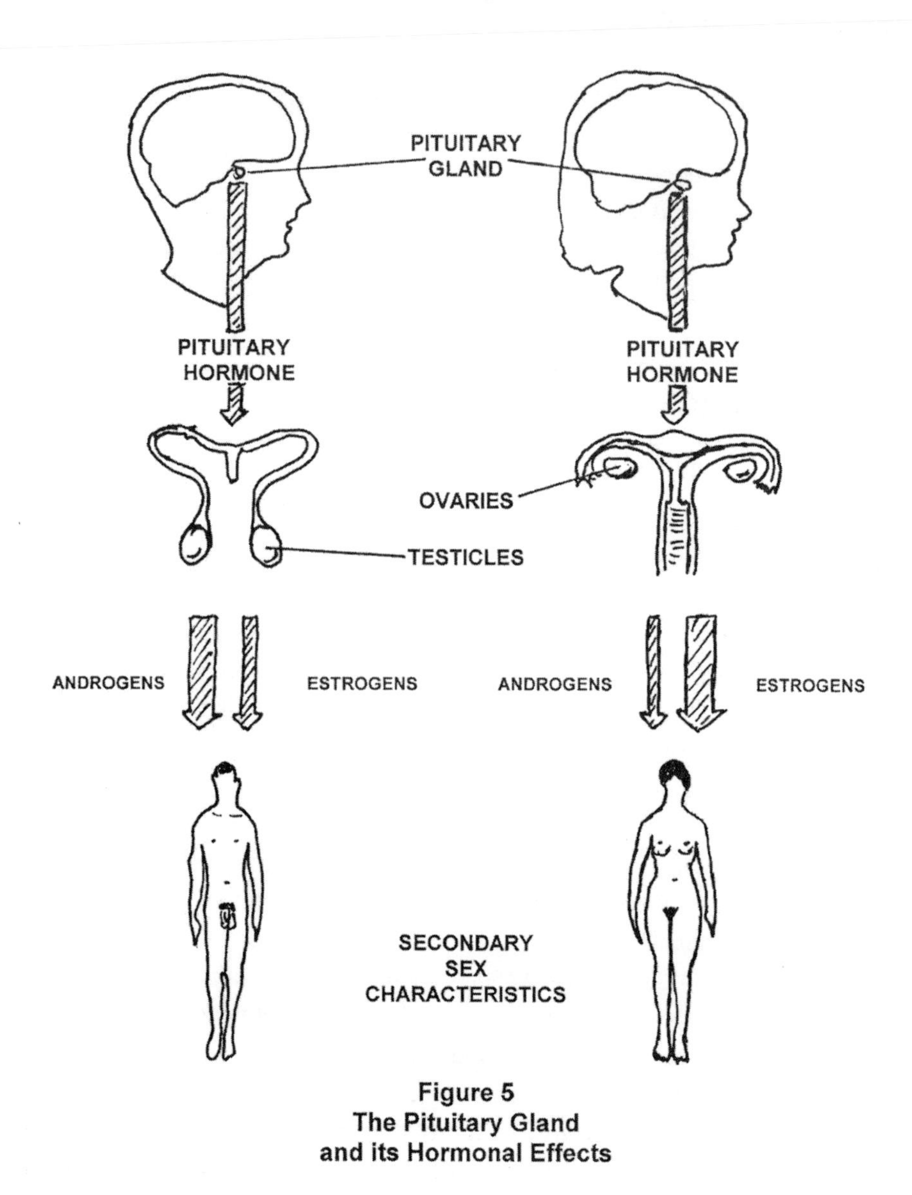

Figure 5
The Pituitary Gland and its Hormonal Effects

Primary Sexual Characteristics

The primary female sexual characteristics are the **ovaries** and the **vagina**. The primary male sexual characteristics are the **testicles** and the **penis**. Figure 6 gives you an idea about the location and appearance of the male and

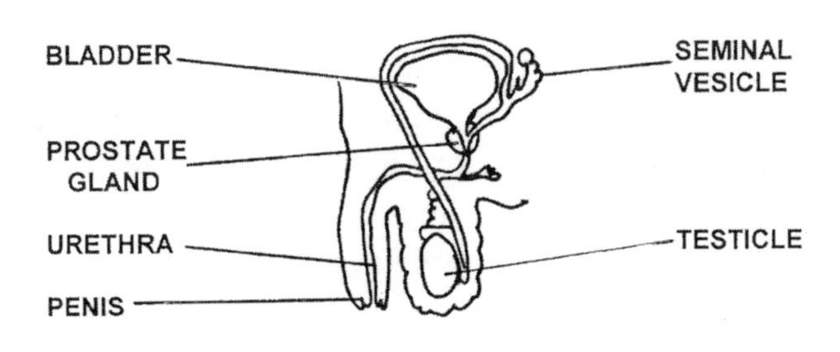

MALE

FALLOPIAN TUBES

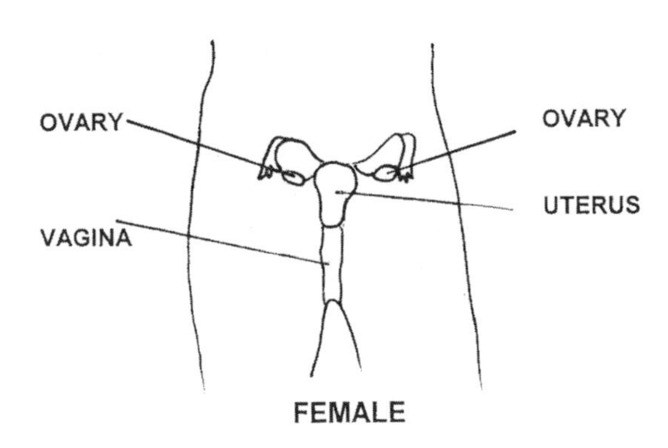

FEMALE

Figure 6
Male and Female Genitalia

female genitals. The first signs of sexual development occur in the testicles and ovaries. The two ovaries are inside the body and cannot be observed. They are the size and shape of almonds. The two testicles are located outside the body, partially behind the penis. Each adult testicle is about one and a half inches long and one inch thick. The growth of the testicles would not be easily recognizable to the untrained eye.

Young people worry about abnormalities. They often ask what would happen if the testicles or ovaries are damaged. If a man or woman lacks a testicle or ovary, the remaining one performs the function of both. Men with one testicle and women with one ovary are perfectly normal in their development and ability to conceive children. If both testicles or ovaries are missing or are damaged, something that is very rare, then the person would need hormonal shots for the rest of his or her life. (Hormones are necessary in order to preserve a person's secondary sexual characteristics, which we will study in Chapter 6.) That person would not be able to produce children of his or her own because the testicles and ovaries produce the cells that transmit life, as we will see in Chapter 5.

The penis and the vagina are also important because they allow the transmission of life to take place between the mother and the father. The penis and the vagina usually produce more curiosity than the testicles and ovaries and they will be studied in greater detail in Chapters 7 and 8.

After puberty is already underway by one or two years, the male testicles are able to produce **sperm cells**, or **spermatozoids**. The female ovaries contain thousands of **egg cells** from birth. After puberty is underway the female ovaries begin to release the egg cells, or **ovum**. The sperm cells and egg cells are the ones capable of transmitting life.

5

The Act of Sexual Love

How does life inside the mother begin? The story must be told in several parts because it is God's most wonderful and delicate creation. Let us take a look at God's plan for the union of a sperm and an egg cell before moving on to other more detailed explanations of sexual development.

The story begins at the altar of God when a man and a woman bless their love through the Sacrament of Matrimony. Jesus explained it this way:

> Have you not read that from the beginning the Creator 'made them male and female' and said, 'For this reason a man shall leave his father and mother and be joined to his wife, and the two shall become one flesh?' So they are no longer two, but one flesh. Therefore, what God has joined together, no human being must separate. (Mt. 19: 4-6)

Husbands and wives are committed to love one another and to create life out of their mutual love. In his wisdom, God gave them each a gender and different sexual organs that are complementary (i.e., their body parts actually fit into one another to make them one). Each spouse by himself or herself is not capable of giving life to a baby. God planned it very carefully to make sure that life could only be made by a man and a woman together. The sperm and egg cells must unite in order for life to exist. In other words, not only are cells being united, but so have a man and a woman united themselves to each other in marriage.

A man and a woman declare at their wedding ceremony their intention to be committed to one another and to their future family. After the new husband and wife celebrate their mutual love through the sacrament of Matrimony with their family and friends, they usually go away together. This time away is usually called a "honeymoon." The honeymoon is a time in which the newly married couple can become physically, emotionally, and spiritually intimate without worries or time constraints. It is from this time forward that they engage in the act of **sexual love**, also called **sexual intercourse.** In the act of sexual intercourse, the spouses continually pledge their love to each other. Sometimes this act of love produces life, and the wife becomes pregnant. In this sacred, life-giving act of love, the penis deposits millions of microscopic sperm cells inside the vagina.

The act of sexual love is referred to as **genital sex** because it involves the union of the male and female genitals. Genital sex is reserved for married couples, because genital sexual love is the ultimate expression of the commitment between the spouses who are united in a deep and unconditional love. Genital love between husband and wife provides spiritual, emotional, and physical pleasure:

- **spiritually**, because it is the recognition of the sacramental nature of the sexual act, which fills the spouses with God's grace;
- **emotionally**, because it is the deepest expression of the romantic love between a man and a woman; and
- **physically**, because it is physiological pleasure expressed through an **orgasm**.

An **orgasm** is the climax or final burst of sexual pleasure that the wife and the husband experience at the end of the sex act. The orgasmic pleasure is accompanied by the release of muscular and nervous tension in men and women. It is at the time of the male orgasm that the **ejaculation**, or release of the sperm cells into the vagina, takes place. There is no comparable ejaculation in the female orgasm. Egg cells are released by the ovary about once a month, as part of a woman's **menstrual cycle**, and independently of the act of sexual love. The menstrual cycle will be studied in Chapter 7.

Genital sex is also reserved for those who are married because sexual intercourse can create a new life that is best supported by two parents committed to one another through the marital sacrament. Genital sex outside marriage produces a moral disorder in the human family. Faith-filled Christians, wishing to protect this principle of love and life, teach that genital sex outside marriage

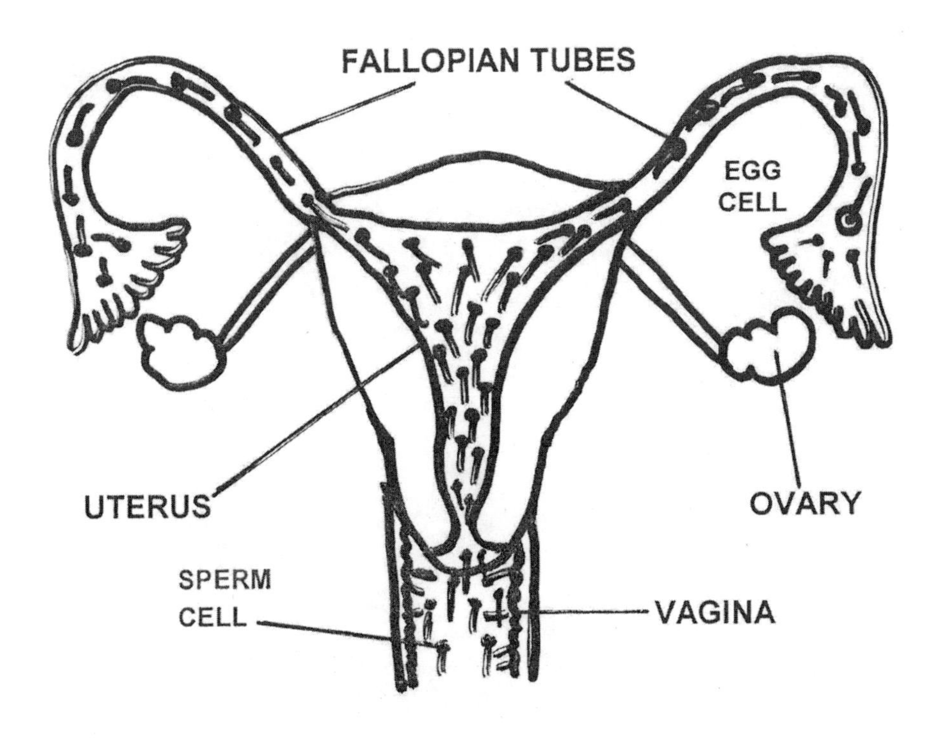

Figure 7
The Meeting of the Sperm and Egg Cells

is sinful. Genital sex includes all actions between a man and a woman that involve contact with the genitals of the other, and which may lead to sexual intercourse.

Each time there is an act of sexual love, the male sperm cells look for an ovum inside the female body. As can be seen in Figure 7, the tiny sperm cells advance through the uterus and the fallopian tubes. If the sperm cells find an egg cell, one sperm cell may unite with it to form the first cell of the new human person, as shown in Figure 8. The sperm cell in Figure 8 is very enlarged, but in reality sperm cells are very microscopic. By contrast, the ovum is the largest cell found in the human body, being about the size of the tip of a pin.

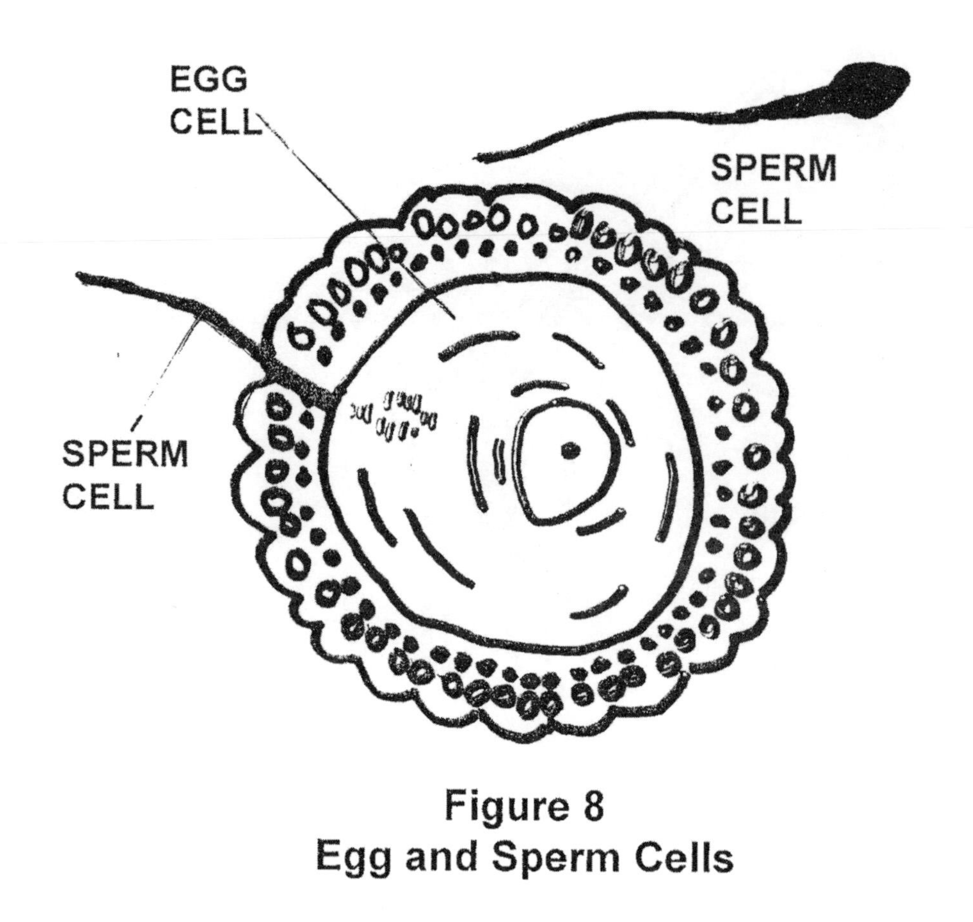

Figure 8
Egg and Sperm Cells

Each cell has exactly one-half of the respective parent's genetic makeup to pass on to the child.

Pregnancy takes place through an act of sexual intercourse in which a sperm cell unites with the egg cell, forming the first cell of the new human person. A common question is how the **gender** of the baby is determined. All egg cells are the same; they are **X**-type cells. Sperm cells, on the other hand, are half X- and half **Y**-type cells. If an X egg cell unites with an X sperm cell the baby will be a girl. If an X egg cell unites with a Y sperm cell the baby will be a boy. As you can see, the father determines the gender of the baby. The selection is random (i.e., there are equal chances that the baby may be a boy or a girl).

X SPERM CELL ***from*** **MAN + X EGG CELL** ***from*** **WOMAN = BABY GIRL**

Y SPERM CELL ***from*** **MAN + X EGG CELL** ***from*** **WOMAN = BABY BOY**

And what about twins? Sometimes when an egg and sperm cell first unite, the cell divides into two identical cells through a process called mitosis that you will study further in biology. This division can only happen with the first fertilized cell, and the result will be **identical twins**. Identical twins share the same gender and physically look the same.

Normally in a woman's cycle—as we will study later—one egg cell is released by the ovary each month. Sometimes the ovary releases two or more egg cells. If each egg cell is fertilized by a sperm cell, the result will be **fraternal twins**. If more than two egg cells are fertilized, the mother could be pregnant with **triplets** (three), **quadruplets** (four), **quintuplets** (five), or more babies. Fraternal twins or triplets may have a different gender, and may not look any more alike than any other biological brother or sister.

It is important to note that all egg cells are fertilized approximately at the same time, not on different months. All develop inside the mother during the same period of time, and all are born at the same time. Also, when the mother is holding more than one baby in her womb, each baby has its own amniotic sac, umbilical cord and placenta, and each is fed by the mother independently of one another. At the time of birth, babies come out one at a time until they are all born.

6

Secondary Sexual Characteristics

In Chapter 4, we learned that the pituitary hormone activates the work of the male's testicles and the female's ovaries. These organs then release androgen and estrogen hormones, which are responsible for the appearance of secondary sexual characteristics in the bodies of boys and girls, respectively (see Figure 5).

Most often, the first noticeable sign of puberty is **pubic hair**, the one universal secondary sexual characteristic. All men and women of all races have pubic hair. It grows above and on the sides of the genitals. At first it consists of straight, short strands of hair without any particular color. Later on, the hair becomes thicker and curls, and tends to assume the color of the eyebrows. The pubic hair of both genders forms a pad around the genitals.

Some men and women also develop **leg hair** and **axillary hair** (which appears under the armpit). In addition, some men develop **facial hair**, **chest hair**, and even hair on their backs. In American culture, women tend to shave their legs and armpits, and many men shave their faces. This is not true in many other cultures, where custom may dictate that hair should not be shaven for either women or men. We should study cultural differences so we can learn to appreciate and respect them. Mockery and ridicule are not acceptable. We also need to work against feelings of repulsion, since beauty depends on cultural values. What may be repulsive to one person or culture may be attractive to someone else.

Hair characteristics are inherited from our ancestors and often depend on which part of the world they came from. For example, people from Southern Italy, France, or Spain tend to develop more body hair than people from northern European countries. Blond men and women who have fair skin tend to develop less body hair than people with darker hair. American Indians tend to develop less body hair. People from some African countries develop a lot of body hair while others have very little or none at all. In general, Asians do not develop a lot of body hair. The color and amount of head hair is also inherited, but unrelated to sexual development.

You cannot be like the next boy or girl. You need to be yourself and learn to appreciate who you are. You are entitled to be curious and to think about differences, but you should avoid making comparisons. Some boys would like to have more body hair because they think it is more manly. Other boys worry that they have too much body hair and think it makes them look ugly. Some girls would like to have less body hair because they think it is more feminine. No one sh ould think they are more or less masculine or feminine, or attractive or unattractive, because of body hair. As your body goes through rapid changes, you may feel insecure and unsure about how you will look afterwards. It takes a while for the changes to be complete and to get accustomed to your newly acquired, post-pubertal, adult body.

During puberty, there is an increase in **muscle development** for boys and girls, although in the end the boys' muscles tend to develop more than the girls' muscles. For example, if we compare two thirteen-year-olds, one who has gone through puberty and one who has not, the one who has gone through puberty will probably be stronger. **Voice changes**, especially noticeable in boys, are also related to puberty. These two changes also worry early adolescents. Some teens worry that the pitch of their voice is too high or too low. Their concerns are related to what they think is more attractive or more common to their gender. There is not much that can be done about these or other physical characteristics. Some guys have a higher pitch throughout their lives, and some girls have a lower pitch. Some people are also stronger than others. Keep in mind that these are *secondary* sexual characteristics. It is the *primary* sexual ones that determine one's gender!

The development of the female **breasts**, along with pubic hair, is a clear indication that a girl is entering puberty. Before puberty, the chests of boys and girls appear to be the same, since both have two nipples that are round and of a different color and texture than the rest of the chest. However, inside the body there is a major difference: the girls have developing **mammary glands** and the boys do not. At the beginning of puberty, girls' breasts begin to bud, making the difference between boys' and girls' chests an obvious one.

The size of adult women's breasts varies from small to large. While the breasts of a young girl are developing, sometimes one breast grows faster than the other, producing unnecessary tension for that girl. Usually those differences disappear during the later years of adolescence, and the difference is only noticeable to the girl herself, not to others around her. Also, the size or shape of a breast, or the nipple of that breast, does not affect the functioning of the mammary glands, which are the significant organs.

Mammary glands look like bunches of miniature grapes with conduits connected to the nipple, as can be seen in Figure 9. These glands produce milk to feed a newborn baby. When a girl is developing into womanhood, her breasts do not contain milk. When that woman marries and becomes pregnant, her mammary glands are not yet activated. When the mother gives birth to a baby, a message is sent to the mammary glands, through hormonal fluids, to begin producing milk. Babies are born with the ability to suck. As the baby sucks the milk from the mother's breasts, the mammary glands produce more milk. When the baby is older and stops sucking from the mother's breasts, the production of milk stops. The mammary glands will not produce milk again until the next time the mother delivers a baby. Breast milk is only for babies.

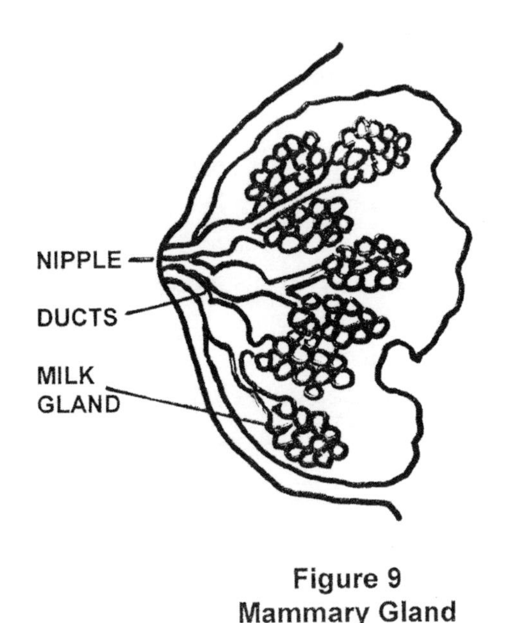

Figure 9
Mammary Gland

Breast-feeding is highly recommended for mothers because the milk they produce is especially designed for their baby and because the feeding enhances the closeness between mother and baby. However, some mothers are unable to breast-feed because they are unable to produce milk, or because the milk they produce cannot satisfy the baby's hunger. Some mothers choose not to breast feed because of work or family responsibilities. Breast-feeding takes time and is a task that cannot easily be shared with a husband or other family members. Mothers are encouraged to breast-feed their babies; however, those who choose not to breast-feed should not be criticized. Adoptive mothers did not go through the process of biological birth, therefore they have no milk in their breasts with which to feed the baby. In cases where breast-feeding is not possible, medical science has advanced formulas that imitate the composition of breast milk so babies can grow healthily.

A word about **hygiene** before moving on. Hygiene is the practice of good health habits. When boys and girls reach puberty, their hormonal changes may produce offensive body odors, especially after sweating. Good hygiene includes taking a daily bath or shower with a generous supply of soap and water. Genitals, backs, armpits, and feet are especially vulnerable to bad odors. Boys and girls should learn to use deodorant on a regular basis, to wear clean clothes after bathing, and to wash their dirty clothes before wearing them again.

7

Specific Pubertal Changes in Girls

Female Genitalia

The female genitalia, or **vulva**, is very private. From the outside, only a line is noticeable. After puberty, that line is surrounded by pubic hair and even the line is not easily seen. The vulva is protected by folds of skin called **major labia** (lips) and **minor labia**. This skin is flexible and able to expand. Figure 10 shows how the expanded vulva would look. Inside the major and minor lips there is the entrance to the **vagina**, which is connected inside the body to the uterus, the fallopian tubes, and the ovaries, as can be seen in Figure 11.

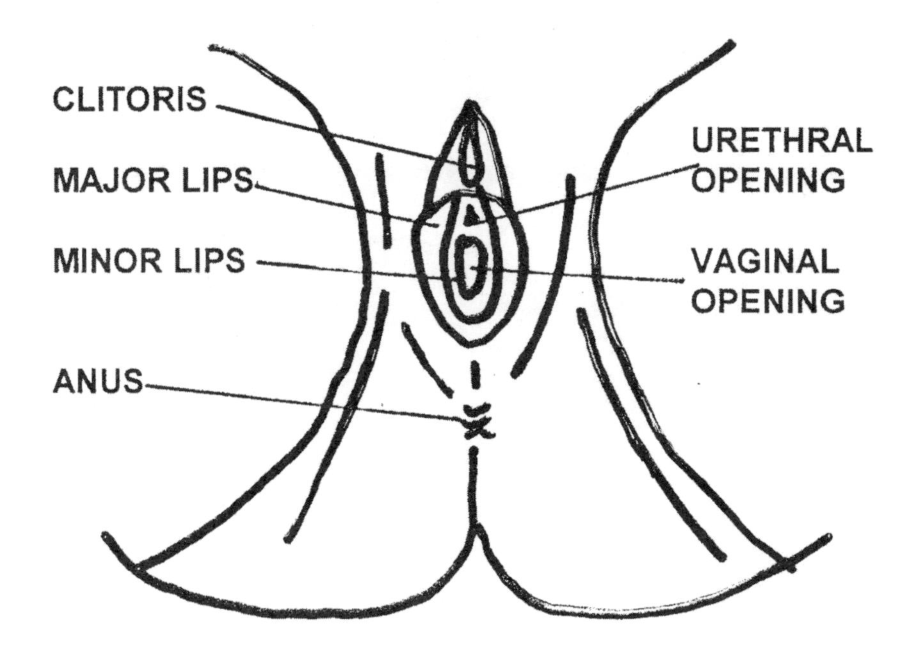

Figure 10
Female Vulva

There is also a **urethra**, which is connected to the **bladder**. It is through this urethral opening that urine passes to the outside. It is important to note that females have two separate systems—one for urination and one for sexuality. Males, as we will study next, only have one system for both.

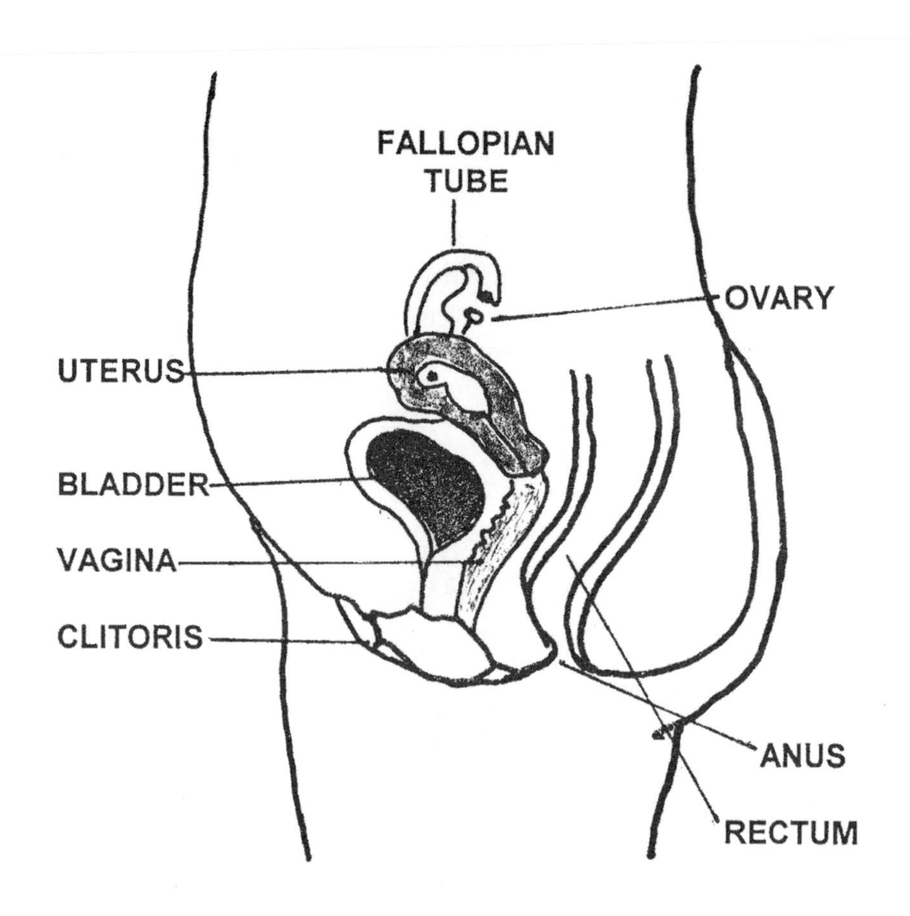

Figure 11
Female Genitalia

The entire genital area, including the entrance to the vagina, has many nerve endings. Nerve endings make the skin very sensitive. These nerve endings are connected to the brain through the spinal cord, so the brain can report pleasurable sensations and experience orgasms. Where the major and minor lips meet there is a ridge of skin called the **clitoris** that has many nerve endings and is a heightened area of sexual stimulation.

Girls are born with a **hymen**. A hymen is a very thin membrane that partially protects the opening of the vagina. The hymen is fragile and may easily rupture through exercise or a medical examination. If still in place at the time of marriage, the hymen will rupture during the first act of sexual love. The rupture may produce discomfort, a quick moment of pain, and some bleeding. The pain quickly disappears and should not interfere with the ongoing act of sexual intercourse (or any such acts in the future). It was once thought that the absence of the hymen meant the woman had already engaged in sexual intercourse. It is important to remember that by the time a woman marries she may not have an intact hymen. These days women are very active, and the absence of the hymen does not mean she has had sexual intercourse before marriage.

Menstrual Cycles

The beginning of a girl's menstrual cycle, or **menstruation**, is probably getting close when her pubic hair begins to appear and her breasts begin to bud. It is called "menstruation" because the process typically occurs on a monthly basis (in Latin, *menstruus* means "monthly"), and some call it a **period** because of this regular occurrence. The purpose of the menstrual cycle is to prepare the woman for pregnancy by providing the uterus with a new lining of tissue each month. This blood-rich tissue lining ensures the life of the newly conceived baby. As the fertilized cell comes into the uterus without an umbilical cord, it needs a nutritious lining in order to develop adequately. Figure 12 depicts the uterus before and after the lining is established.

Let us assume that a young woman is neither married nor pregnant. Her body does not know whether she is going to be pregnant soon, so the uterus maintains its preparations. For a period of roughly fourteen days, nutrient-

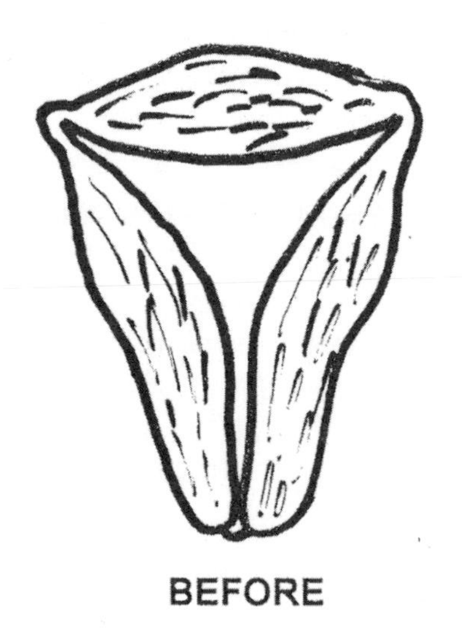

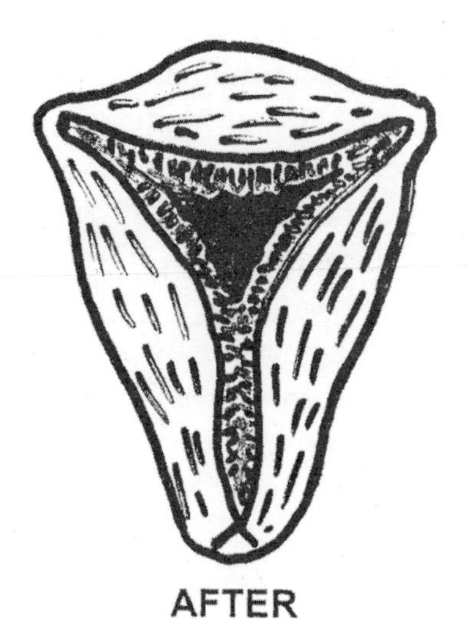

Figure 12
Uterus Before and After Lining is Established

rich blood is deposited on the walls of the uterus. Study the chart in Figure 13. The forming of this lining can take as few as ten, or more than twenty days. Particularly when a girl is young and just beginning to have menstrual cycles, the number of days for the establishment of the lining may vary quite a bit from one month to the next.

Once the lining is in place, say in fourteen days, an egg cell is released from one of the ovaries and passes into the fallopian tube. This process is called **ovulation**. The egg cell lives in the fallopian tube for three days and advances through the fallopian tube and into the uterus. By the time this ovum passes into the uterus, it is either a fertilized cell or a dead cell. Assuming the woman is not pregnant, the dead egg cell continues on its way, moving down through the uterus and birth canal and out through the vagina. This process takes roughly fourteen days.

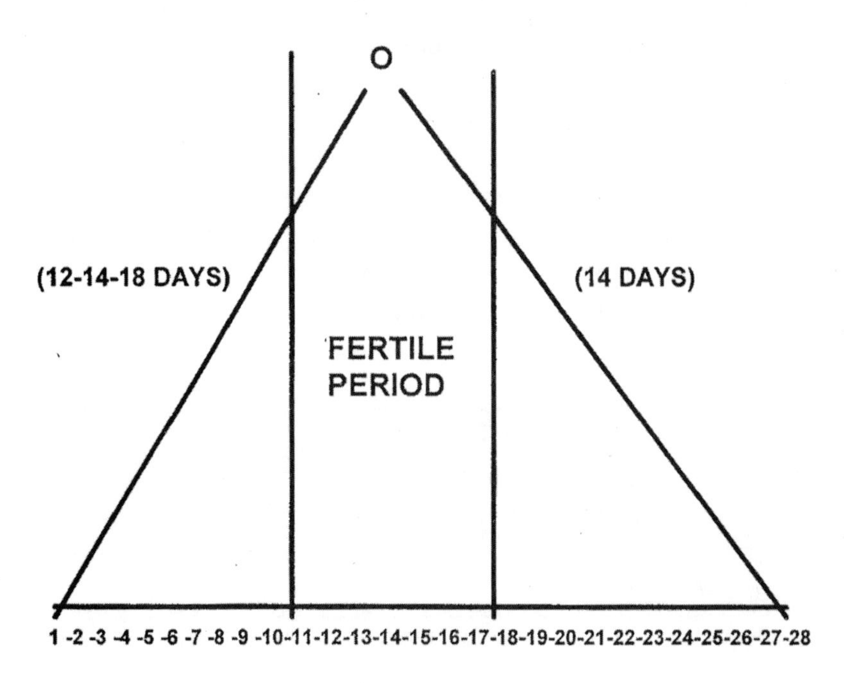

Figure 13
The Menstrual Cycle

By now about twenty-eight days have gone by since the lining was established. The blood cells contained in the uterus have now become dead blood cells. The blood needs to be released and replaced with a new lining of blood cells. As the egg cell passes out of the vagina, the blood that was in the uterus goes with it. The first day that blood begins to be released is the first day of the next menstrual cycle. During the next three to seven days drops of blood and tissue will continue to come out through the vagina while fresh blood cells form the new lining in the uterus. Once the lining is established, another ovulation takes place. This time, the ovum comes from the opposite ovary, and the process repeats itself each month, with ovulation switching each month from one ovary to the other, and with menstruation occuring at the end of each cycle.

The total menstrual flow is about four ounces of blood. The flow resembles a leaky faucet, often with a greater drip on the first day of the period. Since the blood coming out could stain the clothing, the girl needs to protect herself with a **sanitary pad**, or **napkin**, which is often called a "maxi-pad" or "mini-pad." It is simply a very small diaper placed in front of the vagina to gather the drops of blood coming out and keep the woman clean. Some women prefer a **tampon**, which is a cotton swab inserted into the vagina to gather the blood before it comes out. Different families, and even members within the same family, have different preferences. A girl should first consult with her mother about the best product to use. Any product that will help a girl to be clean and hygienic is acceptable; however, douching is considered unnecessary.

Take time, girls, to discuss with your parents which products they prefer and why, and what seems to be more acceptable to you. Some mothers prefer to start you out on a simple sanitary napkin and have you adjust to the product you prefer as you get older and have more experience managing your period.

The exchange of lining inside the uterus often produces cramping, discomfort, and pain. The women who experience discomfort report it is usually worse on the first and second day of their period. If a girl experiences pain, she should tell her parents so they can give her a medication to alleviate it. If the pain is intense, she should consult her doctor to evaluate the problem. In addition, some women experience emotional changes the week before menstruation begins. This **pre-menstrual syndrome** (PMS) is described as feeling moody and cranky. Bad moods should not be automatically labeled as PMS. If a girl thinks she is experiencing PMS, she should discuss it with her parents and her doctor.

At some points during the month, especially before and after the menstrual cycle but unrelated to it, a woman may have a **vaginal discharge**. A discharge is the release of fluid through the vagina. It is the residue of fluid and mucus produced inside the vagina as a natural protection against infection or germs, or as a lubricant prior to the act of sexual intercourse. If the discharge is accompanied by irritation, pain, or itching, it could be the result of an infection that requires medical treatment. A physician should be consulted in those cases. A **yeast infection** is one such common infection in women, not related to sexuality, and is easily treated.

Menstrual cycles occur between puberty and **menopause**, the time when a woman's ovaries stop releasing egg cells and pregnancy is no longer possible. For most women, this happens between the ages of forty-five and fifty.

Women's sexual organs are more complex than men's. One day a woman may become a mother, so she has a uterus in which to host her baby while it is inside her body, and she has breasts with which to feed her baby once the baby is born. Men have neither a uterus nor breasts. In his mysterious wisdom, God placed a lot of responsibility on women regarding motherhood. It is most important that a man learn to truly appreciate his mother, and, later on, his wife. Although a man cannot have a baby himself, he must exercise responsibility by offering his wife physical and emotional support during her menstrual cycles, pregnancy, and the delivery of each baby.

Take time, girls, to discuss your sexual feelings, your feelings about menstruation, and your other concerns with your parents. There is no need to deny your sexual reactions, since every female has them.

8

Specific Pubertal Changes in Boys

Male Genitalia

Males have a **penis** and two **testicles** outside the body. The penis has a double function: one for urination, and the other for sexuality. For the purpose of urination, the penis has a duct inside, the **urethra**, which is connected to the bladder. Urine comes from the bladder and passes to the outside through the urethra. This process has nothing to do with sexuality.

Although urination is not related to sexuality, it is worthwhile to mention here that some boys (girls, too) are **bedwetters**. They typically developed a bad habit when they were little by urinating in their bed while asleep. As they got older they sometimes had accidents at night. Since, in the boys' case, the penis is the organ through which the urine passes, these boys begin to think there is something wrong with their sexual organ. Bedwetters need to be reassured that they will overcome this bad habit in time. They should also understand that it has nothing to do with their sexuality or sexual development.

My advice to bedwetters is to go to the bathroom before going to sleep, and at any time that they wake up during the night. Again, a medical evaluation may be helpful, particularly when there are lots of concerns on the part of the child or the parents. I ask those who do not wet their bed to please refrain from making fun of siblings or friends who struggle with the habit. They are not fully responsible for it, and mockery is cruel.

For the purpose of sexuality, the male has two testicles that begin to produce sperm cells one to two years after he has reached puberty. The testicles are protected inside a membrane called the **scrotum**. The scrotum can be thin and loose, with the testicles hanging farther from the body. The scrotum can also be very tight and thick and the testicles very close to the body. The differences depend on temperature and emotion. For example, when it is

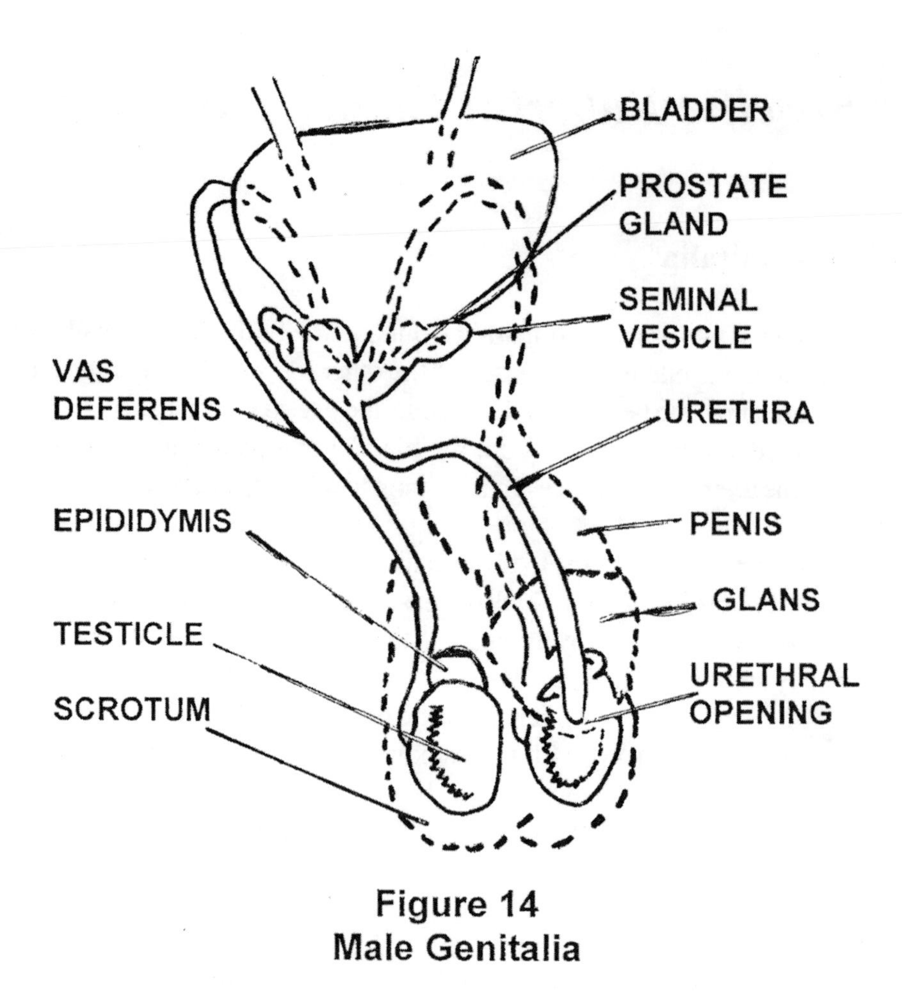

Figure 14
Male Genitalia

very cold, or when a man is scared, the scrotum usually thickens and retracts into the body to protect the testicles. The body attempts to maintain an ideal temperature for the testicles and uses closeness to the body to accomplish it.

Often one testicle is slightly larger than the other, usually the left one. Figure 14 shows how each testicle has an **epididymis**. The epididymis is a mass of tiny tubes attached to the testicle where the sperm cells are stored. Millions of sperm cells are continually produced in the testicles, unlike the cyclical pattern of the ovary which releases an ovum once per cycle.

Figure 14 also shows how each testicle is connected to a conduit called the **vas deferens**. The vas deferens is responsible for carrying the sperm cells out of each testicle. There are two vasa deferentia that pass first through the two **seminal vesicles,** and then through the **prostate gland**. These two organs produce a fluid called **semen**.

Semen is a thick, sticky, yellow-white fluid. Each ejaculation of semen is one to two teaspoons-full that contains two hundred million to five hundred million microscopic sperm cells. The sperm cells mix with the semen and come out through the urethra. The semen coats the urethra to protect the sperm cells from the uric acid left by the urine, which would kill the sperm cells. The ejaculation of semen also facilitates the delivery of sperm cells into the vagina, cervix, uterus, and fallopian tubes.

Some boys are concerned as to whether or not urine and semen can pass through the urethra at the same time. The answer is no, this cannot happen at the same time. As urine comes out of the bladder, it pushes a valve that closes off the vasa deferentia. As semen is ready to pass, the same valve closes off the conduit coming from the bladder.

The urethra is located at the center of the penis. The penis is composed of tissue that has no bone, and no cartilage like the nose has. Basically, the penis is expandable skin and tissue that surrounds the urethra, with an opening at the end of the urethra called the **meatus**. As can be seen in Figures 14 and 15, the penis has a **glans**, which is the farthest tip from the body. Between the glans and the rest of the penis there are many nerve endings, connected to the brain through the spinal cord. These nerve endings make the penis very sensitive and capable of experiencing pleasurable sensations and orgasms.

The tissue that surrounds the urethra is a spongy type of tissue called the **cavernous body**. Blood vessels allow the blood to flow into the cavernous body. The penis becomes large, stiff, and erect as the blood fills the spongy tissue. This enlargement is called an **erection**. Sometimes the penis is not completely straight, with a tendency to turn slightly to one side, especially when erect. All males experience erections throughout their lifetime. A baby boy can be born with an erection, and as he grows he will at times experience

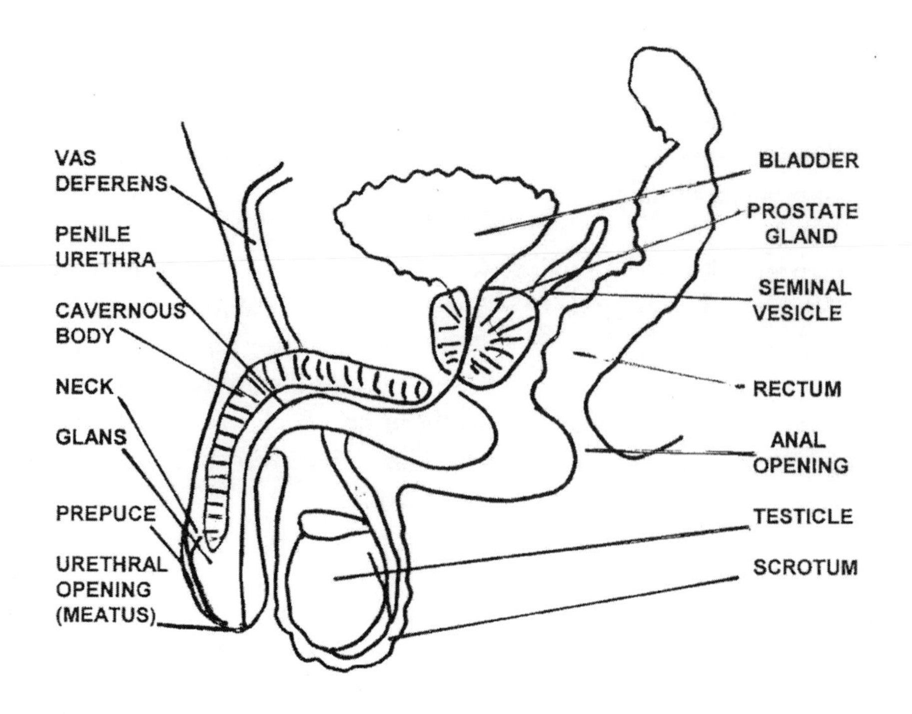

Figure 15
Male Genitalia

them. The stiffness can appear or disappear in seconds as the blood enters or leaves the penis. These erections may or may not be related to sexuality. Erections are often unrelated to sexual stimulation, particularly when a boy is small, or as he develops from boyhood to manhood. Erections may also be related to sexual feelings and desires. A sexual erection makes the physical aspect of sexual love possible, facilitating the entry of the penis into the vagina.

Guys become curious and concerned about the size of the penis. A penis varies greatly in size from one moment to another, depending on the amount of blood flowing into or out of it, so no particular size would be an accurate measure of the penis. At the point of maximum penile erection, an adult male penis may measure over three to six inches in length. Penis size has nothing to do with race, body size, or sexual capability. The smallest or largest adult penis would find an easy entry into the smallest or largest adult vagina.

When a man experiences an erection, the testicles, seminal vesicles, and prostate gland prepare for the ejaculation of semen. Since erections are often brief, the message to ejaculate semen is canceled. These canceled messages during the day, or erections while the man is asleep, may contribute to the release of semen in a **nocturnal emission** or **wet dream**. It is called "nocturnal" because people usually sleep at night, and "emission" because the fluid comes to the outside. It is also called a wet dream because it is sometimes accompanied by a sexual dream. Be reassured that we always dream; that a dream's context varies; that dreams are complex; and that we are not responsible or morally culpable for what we dream. Many boys report they are unable to remember their dreams—that is normal, too. The release of semen in a nocturnal emission leaves a wetness in the clothing or bedding.

Wet dreams do not occur until the boy has been into puberty for a year or two, and they tend to occur more often in adolescence than in later years. Wet dreams are random and unpredictable, some boys have them often, others rarely. One boy may have two wet dreams one week and not have another one for a year. Another boy may report never having had a wet dream. Nocturnal emissions, if they occur, are normal and moral. Even if a dream was very sexual, a person does not sin in his or her sleep. The next morning a boy should change the linen or underwear if they are stained, and wash himself. He need not be ashamed of wet dreams nor hide them from parents. Parents are aware of wet dreams and clearly understand that a boy is developing into an adult man. Girls do not have wet dreams but they can have sexual dreams too. Neither girls nor boys are responsible for their dreams, no matter how sexual they may be.

At birth, the glans is surrounded by a thin skin called the **foreskin**, or **prepuce**. **Circumcision** is the process of removing the foreskin. Circumcision is optional. Some families think it is good to circumcise a boy for purposes of hygiene, since dirt or dried fluids can accumulate between the foreskin and the glans. Other families believe that if a boy was born with a foreskin, it is the natural way to be, and it should be left alone. Neither system has been proven to be better than the other. Jesus was circumcised in a religious ceremony on the eighth day after he was born, in accordance with the tradition of the Jewish religion. Christians do not require circumcision. North Americans have practiced circumcision for a long time but other cultures do not circumcise their males. These customs change from time to time. If a boy is not circumcised, he needs to pull back the foreskin until the glans is totally uncovered, and wash it well every time he showers. Parents of uncircumcised boys need teach them the proper hygiene of the penis from the time they are very young.

Take time, boys, to discuss your sexual feelings, your feelings about circumcision and wet dreams, or your other concerns with your parents. There is no need to deny your sexual reactions, since every male has them.

9

Growing Up Private and Curious

It often happens that as boys and girls approach puberty they develop a greater need for privacy. Perhaps this need for privacy arises because their bodies are changing and they are beginning to be more aware of their sexual feelings, or because they are more self-conscious about their physique. Interestingly, at the same time that they wish for more privacy they also become more curious about the appearance, physique, and sexual development of others around them. If you have experienced these feelings, please understand they are quite normal.

A desire for privacy is normal, but sometimes the need for excessive privacy may be related to your insecurities and embarrassment, and based on a feeling that your physical development is not adequate. Actually, what may help increase your level of security the most is to have a parent or a doctor check your physical development. By overcoming your need for privacy and your fear of exposure, you allow a parent or doctor to confirm that you are growing up healthily. I strongly recommend you ask your parents or your doctor questions about sexual development even when the adult has not made any comments about it. Although asking questions could be uncomfortable for a moment, in the long run it will ease doubts and help you feel more confident about your development.

The issue of privacy requires a sense of balance. Parents should be aware of the increased need for privacy of their pubertal son or daughter. It is important to knock, wait for a response, and allow some time to pass before entering a teen's room. All parents need to exercise prudence when dealing with early adolescents, especially mothers with their sons and fathers with their daughters. Teens must not become excessively preoccupied with privacy, nor or should they use it to avoid interacting with their parents. Teens should remain open to their parents and make every effort to trust them without restrictions. A few puberty changes are not the end of the world. Remember, teens, that your parents have changed you and bathed you since you were born. They rejoice in your growth, and you need their support, guidance, and supervision while growing up. Honestly, I recommend that you parents not grant your teens total privacy.

Take time to discuss your need for privacy with your parents. I must tell you, I am against locked doors or rules forbidding parents from entering rooms. I am, however, in favor of respect and sensitivity when teens are changing or using the bathroom. Each family is unique and has unique standards. After the discussion, please feel free to disregard my recommendations and function according to the rules you all feel most comfortable with.

I think it is also beneficial to reflect on the fact that what may be commonplace in your home may not be so in other homes. Be sensitive to your friends' needs when they come to your home to sleep overnight or for an extended period of time. At the same time, be prudent when you visit others' homes so you may respect their style and values without betraying your own. I recommend that you develop such a high level of communication with your parents that you can call them at any time if you are uncomfortable and feel you need to be picked up somewhere. The fact that you feel uncomfortable does not mean that the family you are with should be judged as bad or sinful. However, their ways may be unfamiliar to you and it is probably better that you go home to at least discuss the situation with your parents and obtain their advice.

At the same time that you may experience a need for greater privacy you may also become more curious. Curiosity about the physical appearance and sexual development of men and women alike, independent of your gender, is normal when the person is growing up. You were born **nude**, without clothes—that was your "birthday suit." It is healthy to be clothed: after birth, babies are put in diapers to keep them clean and warm. Once clothed, the opportunity to observe the sexual organs of others disappears. It is normal to feel curious; it is part of learning. If you have not seen something and the opportunity arises, you are probably going to look. The chance to look usually comes only when people are changing at home or in locker rooms. It is not sinful to look incidentally in those circumstances, and you should not feel guilty about it. However, you should recognize that the other person deserves respect and privacy. Even if he or she chooses to change openly, you should not prolong your stare. It is wrong to invade others' privacy and to seek opportunities to observe others' nudity.

Curiosity sometimes leads a young person to look for other opportunities beyond those just described. One sad example is **pornography.** Pornography consists of books and song lyrics that talk about sex, and pictures, magazines, videos, and movies that show nudity and present scenes with sexual acts. Pornography abuses your natural curious needs and presents material that encourages sexual feelings and reactions. Pornography confuses the appreciation of the beauty of the gift of sexuality because much of the material is gross and offensive. It also confuses your knowledge about physical development and physique by presenting only a very small range of men and women who possess specific body types. Most people do not look like those few men and women who are paid to take advantage of others' curiosity and sexual desire by posing or performing in the nude.

Pornography does not treat the issues of love and sexuality respectfully or accurately. It leads to more thoughts and desires for sex than are necessary. The visual images remain imprinted in one's memory and distort the ideals and purpose of sexuality.

I am also concerned that the exposure to graphic pictures or videos of sexual acts may produce doubts about sexuality. Young people lack experience, and curiosity will lead to observing both the person of the opposite and the same sex. Although the curiosity is normal, it has worried and confused many young people. Some worry about the normalcy of their developing body in comparison to the bodies of adults they see in pornographic pictures. Others worry that they have paid too much attention to the person of the same sex.

Some teens show off their interest in pornography because they think it makes them sound more mature and experienced. In reality they are only exposing their insecurities. Some fake their distaste for that kind of material in an effort to fit in and become popular. Others can hardly keep themselves away from pornography and find it pleasurable. Keep in mind that pornography can become addictive, and that addictions are hard to overcome. The latest wave of pornographic material is being accessed through the Internet. It is so easy to access this material that some young people find it difficult to avoid; parents should discuss these issues and take the necessary supervisory steps. You must stay away from all pornographic materials and keep in mind that when your parents supervise you, or even intrude on your privacy, they are helping you grow up a to be a whole and more healthy person.

I wish to challenge both adults and teens to resist the curiosity to look at pornography and to get rid of any pornography they may have. This includes what is now called "soft" pornography, such as underwear and swimsuit advertising. Pornography is neither soft nor hard, it is simply a negative influence on everyone it touches.

Pornographic material can lead to sinfulness, and one's participation in producing, distributing, or posing for sexually explicit or suggestive material is also sinful for many reasons, not the least of which is its power to tempt others. Jesus was very forceful when challenging people not to scandalize or lead others to sin (Mt 18:6).

I often tell young people: "You are the victims of pornography. You did not participate in the creation of this material, adults did. Do not support their bad business. You would not want to see your mother or father, sister or brother, posing or acting this way. Take a stand against an industry that desecrates the gift of sexuality." As children grow older they learn more about their bodies and the bodies of others in a natural and spontaneous way. Those unable to stop looking at pornography should find the support they need to overcome this tendency or addiction.

Curiosity sometimes leads children and teens to explore their bodies' sexual feelings and reactions. Prolonging thoughts about sex or purposely touching the genitals can produce a sexual reaction. If the exploration continues, the sexual reaction increases in intensity and reaches an orgasm. The experimentation of sexuality alone, accompanied by an orgasm, is called **masturbation**. In the case of boys, the sexual reaction produces an erection of the penis, and after puberty the orgasm is also accompanied by the ejaculation of semen.

Kids may discover masturbation accidentally during early childhood or later on during adolescence. They may also discover it through conversations with other children or teens, or through pornography. If done repeatedly for a long time, masturbation can become a bad habit which may be difficult to overcome. Masturbation occurs more often among adolescent boys than girls, perhaps because the male sexual organs are outside and experience erections. Some people teach that masturbation is part of development and is an acceptable behavior; others question the validity of that perspective, especially because masturbation may become compulsive (i.e., addictive).

It is important to remember once again that the purpose of sexuality is life and love. Masturbation does not lead toward either end and therefore it is a disordered behavior. The young person should make every effort to appreciate his or her sexual feelings and avoid this type of experimentation. Morally, a disordered behavior is sinful, not part of God's plan. However, God is most understanding of young people who are struggling to understand and regulate their gift of sexuality. God continually loves, forgives, and encourages children and teenagers to remain faithful to him. He wants them to recognize their call to holiness and the difficulty of mastering their sexuality.

It is particularly difficult to regulate sexual desires if masturbation began in childhood and has gone on for several years. Some young people get discouraged when they hear that the behavior is disordered and feel unable to stop masturbating. If masturbation has been or is currently a problem for a particular teen, I try to emphasize that the difficulty should not be a source of shame or embarrassment. Masturbation often begins without the person fully realizing what he or she is doing; it is often associated with curiosity and impulsivity; and it is rarely intended to offend God. Masturbation does not cause any physiological impairment, and it is less emotionally harmful if the person is not too preoccupied, ashamed, or depressed about it. On the other hand, no one should give up making every effort to regulate their sexual feelings and impulses, in order to fully appreciate God's gift of sexuality. Practicing the virtue of **chastity** is most helpful in regulating sexual desires. The next chapter will be dedicated to study the virtue of chastity.

> **Take time** to discuss issues of pornography with your parents. Agree that there will be no anger or punishment on this or any other topic you discuss. Be honest about what you have seen accidentally or consistently, through friends or at home. Some parents keep pornography at home, some even openly. You need to challenge them about it. There should be no pornography in your home. This is also a good time to talk about masturbation, a most delicate and difficult subject for parents and teens to discuss. In this and other tough subjects, you may want to begin with a prayer. God's grace may facilitate your openness.

Curiosity may sometimes lead children and teens into **sexual experimentation**. They may have played "doctor," or dared each other to "show you mine if you show me yours." Older children may have played "spin the bottle" or "truth or dare" games. Sometimes the play leads to touching, kissing, or acting in sexual ways. Children usually hide in order to play this way. Most of the time they deny doing it and end up feeling guilty about it. Sometimes a person who has been involved in sexual experimentation talks to his or her peers with pride, and if the others have not been involved in any sexual experimentation, they may feel as if they have lost out on some fun. I want to stress to those who have not experimented that they have not missed out on anything; they do not have to deal with the possible fears, tension, confusion, or guilt usually associated with sexual experimentation.

I want to assure those who have sexually experimented, even minimally, that they can grow up all right, no matter what their curiosity or imagination has led them to do. Some children have experimented just once or a couple of times, others repeatedly for years. Some have experimented with a child of the same sex, others with a child of the opposite sex. In either case, there does not have to be any bad, long-term consequences. However, these children need to face what they have been involved in and have the courage to share it with their parents. If it is too hard to share it with parents first, then it should be shared with another trusted adult. If that is still too hard, then counseling may be helpful to understand the behavior and overcome fears or guilt.

When an adult or older teen engages a younger child or teen in sexual activity, that is not sexual experimentation. It is **sexual abuse**. Sexual abuse may or may not be violent or forced. Some adults can trick or coerce a younger person into cooperating by abusing his or her curiosity, innocence, or ignorance. A child should not feel responsible for an adult's actions, even if they have agreed with the adult or encouraged the behavior after they learned it. Adults have enough knowledge to guide, manage, and control a child's behavior. In other words, it is the abuser's sin. The one abused is the victim.

The only adults who should touch a child's genitals are the child's parents or other close relatives who help bathe or clothe the child, or the child's doctor in the examination room. Adults or older teens who have purposely touched, played with, or even asked a child to touch their genitals have committed sexual abuse. Any person who remembers an experience of sexual abuse, even if it is considered minimal, should tell his or her parents. No matter what consequences this revelation may bring about, it is most important to share all incidents of sexual abuse with them or another trusted adult.

Sexual abuse can produce shame, guilt, and confusion. The best remedy is to talk about it and receive assurance from loved ones that it was not the victim's fault. Some young people continue to feel they were at fault even after sharing an incident or pattern of abuse and discussing it. Those people need to remain honest about their doubts and continue to talk about the incident or series of incidents they experienced. Peace will follow after a while. Sexual abuse is most harmful when it is hidden. Once the experiences are discussed, the bad feelings begin to go away little by little.

Those young people who have not been sexually abused should be assured that a clear understanding of sexual abuse is the best way to prevent it from happening to them in the future. They should pray for those who have not been as fortunate, so that victims of sexual abuse may have the strength to share the truth with their parents or some other responsible adult they can trust.

Take time, a long time, a prayerful time, to discuss the issues of sexual experimentation and abuse. Here, more than ever, you need reassurance from your parents. *Would you be mad if I had something to share with you? Would you tell the person or persons it happened with, or anyone else, without my permission? Would you distrust or dislike me?* If you have something to tell them and have received these assurances, give it your best effort. It is really difficult! You may still not be totally sure your parents can handle it, and crying is common for you *and* them in this kind of situation. Parents, please recognize this is a hard exercise, and that if there has been sexual experimentation or abuse, your son or daughter will need to be reassured of your love many times. The issue must be revisited a week and a month later—as many times as it is needed—after the original discussion takes place. Counseling may be necessary, depending on the complexity of the issues discussed and particularly if the child must be challenged to allow confrontation or legal action against those involved.

10

The Virtue of Chastity

Chastity safeguards authentic love.—Pope John Paul II

From birth, human beings can experience sexual feelings and reactions. As we grow older, we become capable of forming mental images, remembering situations and events, and thinking about sexuality. Sexual thoughts can lead to desires, which, when mixed with physical reactions, can lead toward sexual actions. Human actions need to be regulated by moral principles in order to protect people in our society. For example, society considers stealing immoral because people's property needs to be protected. Sexual behavior must be regulated in accordance with sexual morality; Christian sexual morality aims to protect individual dignity and the institution of the family. The proper control of our sexual thoughts and actions helps us fulfill our need for intimacy and love while protecting the stability and unity of the human family. It is within a lasting, firmly established family unit that the ultimate purpose of sexuality—to promote and protect life and love—is best accomplished.

"Sexuality is indeed a precious gift from God because it involves physical, emotional, intellectual, spiritual, and moral aspects. It is a powerful combination of instincts and learned responses that require guidance and control."

Chastity is the Christian virtue that guides the sexual instincts and helps us develop self-control. It helps us manage our sexual development. Sexuality is indeed a precious gift from God because it involves physical, emotional, intellectual, spiritual, and moral aspects. It is a powerful combination of instincts and learned responses that require guidance and control.

Sexual morality is achieved by practicing chastity. This virtue helps us appreciate and delay sexual gratification until genital sexual actions can be fulfilled by committed spouses within the sacrament of Matrimony. The married couple's sacramental commitment implies their willingness to love one another, and to accept and love the children that will come from their union. Once married, chastity helps them remain faithful to one another.

It is through chastity that we are able to make good decisions that relate, directly or indirectly, to sexuality. We need to recognize that we are:

- **Responsible for what we think.** Yes, we are responsible for our thoughts. Sexual ideas can spring to mind. We need not panic or worry about the fact that such thoughts enter our mind. However, we need to manage our sexual thoughts. Once we are aware of them, it is best to move on to other thoughts, such as projects, hobbies, sports, or other constructive personal interests or challenges. If we stay focused on sexual thoughts, our reactions become more intense and our desire to stop them gets weaker. Consciously consenting, that is, deciding to continue to indulge in the same thoughts, weakens our moral development and is sinful.

> We are called to be holy. Take time to think about God. Thinking about God's love for us and Jesus' sacrifice for us on the cross is called **meditation**. This kind of reflection lifts up our soul and can help us place sexual love in its proper perspective.

- **Responsible for what we see.** Some things are unavoidable and come into our line of sight. We are responsible to stop looking when we are conscious that something is immoral. Pornographic material is a prime example of something we need to avoid. Visual images become stuck in our brains. Long after having seen a sexual image, it may still be clearly visible in a person's mind. Our consent to look at pornography weakens our moral development and is sinful. Even mainstream movies and television shows present skewed images of sexual love that can be confusing and hurtful. Since it is almost impossible to portray the deepest spiritual and emotional aspects of sexual love on-screen, sex scenes almost always obscure the beauty and sanctity of God's great gift. The real depth of the sexual experience is found only within marriage.

We are called to be holy. Take time to see God's creation, to observe and appreciate what is most beautiful: the stars, the planets, a rainbow, a sunset, a flower, a tree, a fish, a bird, a baby's smile. God made it all. He made you. See yourself for what you really are: God's loved one, "the apple of his eye."

- **Responsible for what we talk about.** Sexual jokes and immoral conversations should be avoided. Conversations about sexual experiences and reactions can lead other people to think and act sinfully. Unless we are parents, teachers, or counselors, we are not in a position to inform others about sexual matters. Jokes about a person's physical characteristics, gender, or sexual orientation can hurt his or her positive development. Some people think cut downs sound funny, and even argue they were "just kidding." But such comments weaken the confidence and self-image of the other person. When we accidentally make such comments, we need to apologize. If someone else makes those kinds of remarks, we should try to change the topic of conversation or walk away. When we consent to talk and joke about sexual matters, the decision may be sinful, depending on the subject matter and intent.

We are called to be holy. Take time to talk with God — that is what **prayer** is all about. Sharing our thoughts and doubts with Jesus, our good and bad moments, can help us to remain strong in our faith and our convictions, and refrain from immoral thoughts, talk, and actions.

- **Responsible for where we go and what we do.** When people go to the wrong place at the wrong time with the wrong company, chances are they will behave badly. We should ask what people are doing and where they are going, and be ready to change our plans if we are not sure we understand what is going to happen. With our presence, we condone an immoral activity. Giving our consent to go places where it is likely we will betray our Christian values may be sinful, depending on our knowledge of the situation or of a previous experience where we already know we faltered.

We are called to be holy. Let us go regularly to the right place at the right time, let us go often to church to worship and to participate in the **sacraments**. The sacraments are signs of God's grace in our life and they will give us the strength to live a moral life. If we sin, confession is the way to go! If we wish to be one with Christ, communion is the way to go!

- **Responsible for that to which we read or listen.** Pornography also surfaces in novels and song lyrics. We may not see this kind of material, but it enters our minds and stimulates our thinking. If we keep on reading a pornographic section of a book or listening over and over to a sexually explicit song we should realize that our behavior is disordered. If we are engaged in inappropriate material, we need to move on to more inspiring stories and songs. If we consent to read with the intention to experience sexual thoughts and reactions, our decision is sinful.

We are called to be holy. We should take time to read the **Bible**, which is God's word. We will always find good advice, and challenging but encouraging words. We should also read also the story of saintly and heroic people who are true models to follow. For example: St. Augustine confessed his long life of sexual sins. He came into the Church, became a bishop and died a saint. Maria Goretti, a young Italian girl of this century, died to protect her sexual integrity when she was asked to consent to have sexual relations.

- **Responsible for choosing the people with whom we spend our time.** Often we may need to sacrifice a friendship out of principle when we have tried and failed to develop a positive, moral relationship with that person. I do not want to suggest that we abandon or betray our friends, or condemn them because they talk or act in immoral ways; rather, we make every effort to show them a different way. If they do not change, we certainly cannot follow in their path. Painful as it is, we may pray for the friend, but keep the distance we need to avoid making a moral mistake ourselves. If we consent to be with a friend when his or her action is sinful, our decision may be sinful too.

We are called to be holy. We should look for godly friends who can help us be the best we can be.

> *"A faithful friend is a life-saving remedy, such as he who fears God finds; for he who fears God behaves accordingly, and his friend will be like himself" (Sir 6:16-17).*

We should exert leadership and make our Church's youth community faith-filled and active.

- **Responsible for how we dress**. Modesty in the way we dress means that we choose to wear clothes that are both fashionable and moral. The way we dress is important because if it is sexually provocative it may lead to sexual thoughts and desires in the other person. It is not just the way we dress — modesty goes deeper than that — it is a challenge to develop purity of heart. It is not just a matter of being a little bit better but the challenge to *desire* to be holy.

11

Adolescent Love Relations

Love Relations

God made you out of his infinite love and empowered you to love others. From the moment you were born you were loved. Your parents and relatives held you, caressed you, kissed you, and hugged you. Hugging is wonderful because it gives us a feeling of warmth, closeness, and belonging. It is very difficult to grow up healthily without a generous supply of love. As you grew older, you became capable of loving back and expressing your care toward those who have loved you. I think the picture of a mother holding her baby or a father holding the hand of his child is inspiring because it evokes heartfelt love. None of these expressions of love are connected with genital sex. The word "love" should express the highest degree of care, affection and friendship. Within Christian marriage, love is also expressed in genital sex. I just want to stress that love comprises far more than sexual responses, and that sexual experiences do not *by themselves* constitute a genuine expression of love.

It is great to have good friends while growing up, boys and girls with whom you can share ideas and experiences. It is normal to like and love your friends in a non-sexual fashion. It need not scare you if, during puberty, your intense feelings at times produce a sexual feeling for another person of the same or the opposite gender. As you grow older, these feelings will be clearer and better regulated.

At some point in the process of growing up—from girlhood to womanhood or from boyhood to manhood—people begin to experience feelings of sexual love toward others of the opposite sex. Some boys and girls wish to have a girlfriend or boyfriend early on in junior high. There is nothing wrong with having interest in developing a relationship with a friend of the opposite sex. However, there is also nothing wrong with waiting to develop a romantic relationship until later during high school or college. I love the phrase: *To yourself be true!* If one wants to have this kind of relationship, fine, and if one does not, that is fine, too.

We need not feel pushed by another guy or girl to develop a relationship we are not ready to have. Some young people fake their wishes or personal interests in an effort to fit into a particular crowd, or to pretend they are very grown-up. These young people are not personally ready for a relationship. By faking their interest in having a boyfriend or girlfriend, they confuse themselves and the person they say they like. In the end, they still secretly think they do not really fit, and sometimes even think that they are not sufficiently masculine or feminine.

Humans are unique beings with special interests and attractions. You must respect your development, family upbringing, and personal experiences. Healthy relationships will occur at the appropriate time and without harm to your sexual development. It cannot be said often enough: *To yourself be true!*

During junior high, or even earlier, some adolescents mention to classmates their attraction toward someone of the opposite sex. Peers then tend to make a big deal about this possible love relationship. The reaction is usually due to nervousness and intrigue about the meaning of love. They become excited, ask too many questions, and gossip. The teens who are just beginning to explore new feelings may end up embarrassed by this kind of negative attention. Insecure and self-conscious, they pull away, confuse each other, and break the friendship. It is best not to overreact when a friend expresses a love interest. Likewise, it is best never to act in response to an embarrassment or peer pressure. It is best to discuss the situation with the person you like.

If a teen has not felt an attraction to a person of the opposite sex within a few years of puberty, they should discuss it with their parents before talking to anyone else. Some young people choose to tell peers, or even strangers on the phone, their worries and concerns about sexual growth, and they end up confused. Parents can help their children sort out their ideas and feelings about sexual attractions. If they think the situation is too complicated, they can find a counselor who can further help their children understand their sexual development.

Take time to discuss with your parents your interests, doubts or concerns regarding relations with other teens. Many teens feel lonely and insecure. It helps to talk about it with someone you trust. Any doubts you may have about masculinity and femininity are best dealt with early on in an open discussion with your kparents.

Dating

As you get interested in having a romantic relationship, you need to keep in mind your moral values and their family's values. Some parents prefer that only older teens date or have exclusive relationships so they do not get too involved in one relationship and have the opportunity to get to know different people. These issues should be discussed to reach healthy compromises. You should be honest and not sneak around. You need your parents' guidance, even when you do not like all of their ideas or find their rules too strict.

Parents, please keep the lines of communication open with your teens. Do not make fun or joke about your adolescent's friends or relationships. Everything is serious and important when one is growing up. Some parents ask about relationships too often, giving the impression that the adolescent should have one. Others preach endlessly against them and make their son or daughter afraid to confide their likes and interests. Be careful not to have a rigid blueprint for their development, but remain consistently strong in enforcing moral values.

Teen relations tend to last longer if the experience does not get too emotionally intense and both parties give each other some space. It may be a sign of too much involvement to have to report to a boyfriend or girlfriend every day at a certain time. It may be too much of an obligation to talk on the phone on a daily basis for a long time. It may be too oppressive not to be able to spend sufficient time with other friends. If the commitment is too serious or the relation possessive, it will tend to break more quickly than if it is properly paced. Interestingly, some teens become possessive because they are afraid that if they don't their relationship will end. In fact, they may be accelerating the break by not giving the necessary freedom to the person they love.

Unfortunately, adolescent relations have great beginnings, but they are fragile and tend to break. If you find yourself anxious that a relationship will break up, let go of the fear. Continually focusing on the fear will not save a relationship and makes the other person unhappy. Most adolescent relations last from a few hours to a few months, although there are always some exceptions to this rule. Keep in mind that the less intense, slower paced, and more moral a relationship is, the longer it tends to last. You should also brace your emotions for possible break-ups. The only love relationship that will last is the one with the person you will marry!

Some young people use the labels "boyfriend" and "girlfriend" as a license to be sexually involved, but if they want a good and moral relationship that can last, they need to prudently regulate their physical expressions of love. A traditional way in which two people in love express their affection for one another is through a **kiss**. A romantic kiss with sexual overtones is an important expression of love. Emotionally, it brings the lovers close to one another; physically, it produces a sexual response. (It is noteworthy that there are more nerve endings in the lips than in the entire body below the waistline.) A kiss should be considered a beautiful expression of love and mutual commitment, and it should not be abused by people who have not even established a relationship with each other as boyfriend and girlfriend. Our society does not seem to value the kiss sufficiently and treats it as unimportant and unrelated to the quality of the commitment of those who kiss.

It should also be kept in mind that there is a "kiss," a "ki-i-i-ss," and then again a "ki-i-i-i-i-ss." Holding hands, hugging, and kissing all have their proper times and places. Each of these expressions can enhance a romantic relationship if used appropriately. If abused, they can lead to genital sexual activity because they tend to produce intense feelings that may lead to sexual intercourse. Genital sex outside marriage will be discussed in the next chapter, but I will point out now that even when there is no intention to have direct genital involvement, the intensity of the "indirect" expressions of love could break down a couples moral controls. Therefore, they need to regulate the frequency and intensity of this activity. If it occurs every time a couple gets together, changes should be made to protect the future and the morality of the relationship. Furthermore, when kissing gets too intense, it is time to stop and take a break. You will know it is intense because you will experience a genital reaction.

I have long told teens that when they are in a situation where their behavior may be **BAD**, they need to seek a **PAL**. Your behavior may be bad if you are bored, alone and in the dark.

B = Bored
A = Alone
D = Dark

Being bored, alone with the person you feel attracted to, and in a dark room, perhaps lit only by a boring TV program, could lead you into a more intense sexual experience than you had originally intended. Instead, find a PAL.

P = People. (You need **people** around whose presence will help keep you accountable and protect you from sexual impulses.)
A = Activities. (You need interesting **activities**. It helps to have a concrete plan about what you are going to be doing with a boyfriend or girlfriend.)
L = **Lights**. A lighted room always helps. Hollywood has taught us to associate romantic relations with dim lights and soft music that set the mood for sexual involvement.

If you take too long to take a break when kissing, you may not have the will power to take a break at all. As your sexual feelings increase, your determination to stop and maintain your Christian sexual values will decrease. The intensity could lead you into more direct expressions of genital sex, and even into sexual intercourse. Reviewing Chapter 10 on the virtue of chastity could help reinforce the importance of your moral values.

You also need to be aware of the consequences of using alcohol and drugs. The use of mind-altering substances is physically and emotionally harmful, and potentially addictive. Their use is illegal for minors and can also significantly reduce your determination not to be sexually involved. Alcohol and drugs cloud moral convictions, encourage carelessness, and may lead to involvement in regrettable activities. I have often heard teens blame alcohol and drugs for their sexual mistakes. They are probably correct in their judgment, and their experience should further alert you to the fact that everyone should stay away from alcohol and drugs.

Young people sometimes attract the attention of the person they like by **flirting**. Flirting may involve making romantic comments, joking, or touching the other person. It can reveal an interest in the other person and even enhance the relationship. However, some people enjoy their own jokes too much and do not realize that they are upsetting the person they are trying to please. Flirting is wrong when it involves demeaning sexual remarks. It is also wrong when it is used to manipulate someone to respond sexually. Playing with someone's mind without the intention to date that person, or on a selfish quest to make one's self feel important, is very wrong.

Boys and girls also need to watch their remarks to peers of the same sex regarding their relationships with members of the opposite sex. Boys may downplay these conversations as "locker-room talk" and girls may simply call it "gossip." But these remarks tend to destroy a person's reputation and contradict any sense of love or care for that person. This kind of talk is particularly bad when it involves exaggerations or lies. It is good to walk away from that kind of conversation or to challenge the person leading it to stop.

13

Chaste Premarital Relations

Most of the ideas in this chapter are taken from my booklet *Healthy Sexual Development—The Key to Chastity*. There I state that the principles of love, life, and commitment to family are best preserved within the sacrament of Matrimony. Waiting to be involved in genital sexual relations until you are married helps maintain an adequate moral order, protects people, and prevents abuses. Beyond these important principles, there are other powerful psychological and moral arguments that favor pre-marital chastity.

Teen love should be a preparation for adult love. After all, teenagers do not remain teenagers forever. Whether we like it or not (and sometimes we may not), we all grow up and become adults. The best way to predict what people will be like tomorrow is to observe how they act today. The ultimate goal is to be able to make a permanent commitment to have a sexual love relationship with one spouse. This goal makes sense because our love needs, and the love needs of the families we establish, are best protected through lifelong relationships.

What is the best preparation for this kind of responsible and committed adult love? The best preparation is years of healthy love experiences within the family and with friends of the same and opposite sexes. Special, non-genital love relationships with one or more persons of the opposite sex during the adolescent and young adult years also prepare us for marriage. In each of these cases, you may invest in relationships that could help you discern your vocation and discover your future spouse. Some adults and adolescents wrongly claim that genital sexual experimentation is good for teens so they can learn about love. They fail to realize that genital sexual behavior should be the *result* of committed love and is not the way to learn about love.

Some teens have been led to believe that they will not be able to love in the future if they do not have sexual relations before marriage. These teens may become resentful, thinking wrongly that their parents are stunting their growth in the most important area of their lives. Not so! Intimate love between committed spouses is what makes genital sexuality a fabulous love experience, transcending and intensifying physical pleasure.

The physical aspect of sex is but a small part of the whole concept of human sexuality. What makes a sexual experience beautiful, satisfying, and growth-promoting, is its relation to:

- **an intense love;**
- **the closeness of the two partners;**
- **the quality of their mutual friendship;**
- **the permanence of their relationship.**

These characteristics only occur together within marriage. Adults are best able to experience meaningful and pleasurable sexual relations when they have carefully learned about the powerful gift of sexuality in non-genital relations during their teen and young adult years.

It is easy, with practical examples from the lives of those around us, to understand the instability of love relations during adolescence. Young people are very excited and joyful at the beginning of every new relationship and become very sad when the relationship ends. In the process, they end up with broken hearts. Though painful, a broken heart is almost a necessary element of growth in the area of love, but the brokenness is severe and detrimental when genital sex was part of the relationship.

Teens are just beginning to learn about love and their love relationships are fragile. As I said in the last chapter, special feelings of love tend to change quickly, lasting from a few hours to a few months. Others may last longer, but these often become "addictive" relationships. This means that the two youngsters, under the banner of "love," become emotionally dependent on each other in an attempt to gain security. In addictive love relationships, the two partners avoid getting to know others or taking risks beyond their own secure boundaries. Often, genital sexual involvement becomes part of the addiction. When these relationships break—and they do—they produce intense pain, sometimes even for the parents who may have also fallen in love with their son's or daughter's friend.

It is worth noting that there are a few exceptional relationships that begin early and lead to a marriage commitment. However, these relationships can be clearly seen as non-addictive, where partners have time to themselves and time to spend with other friends of both sexes. These relationships are also ones in which the partners make conscious efforts to live according to their deep Christian moral values, and to avoid genital sex.

Some teens ask why they should wait until marriage when so many marriages end up in **divorce** anyway. Their argument regarding divorce is not valid. Those who marry at least make the effort to live a lasting commitment. Rarely would two people approach a Christian marriage with the intention to eventually separate and divorce. Personal and emotional problems can contribute to divorce. Flaws in the original decision to get married, such as the immaturity of one or both spouses, or serious differences in their values may also result in a divorce. Rather than using divorce as an argument in favor of pre-marital sex, young people should recognize the complexities of personal commitment and prepare for the responsibility of love and fidelity during their teenage years.

Through their personal pain and mistakes, divorced parents can teach a wonderful lesson to young people about the important elements they need to consider in making a decision to get married. They should also reassure their children about their potential for a successful marriage, and about the beauty and peace that can be found in ultimate commitments and unconditional love.

Both from an emotional and moral point of view, it makes sense to wait until marriage before engaging in genital sex. Let me give you four good reasons why.

First, sex outside marriage can obscure our understanding of true love because sexuality is powerful and pleasurable, and it can make us think we are "in love" when we are really "in lust."

Second, genital sex can add negative pressure and break a love relationship because one or both partners may not be ready for the intense love-response sexual behavior demands. That is, genital sex has been created by God for the act of marriage; the experience itself demands that each partner make a commitment and assume responsibility for the other. We feel bound to one another when we engage in sexual intercourse. I have observed that even in casual sexual relationships, where the element of love was minimal, unsuccessful attempts to make a commitment was the norm.

Third, genital sex can also break the friendship because of the guilt associated with sexual behavior. The well-established teachings of most cultures and religions, Christian and otherwise, recognize the guilt that stems from sexual acts that take place outside the moral order.

On a related point, I think it is sad to see some teens avoiding a quality relationship with a good friend for fear that romantic involvement will destroy the friendship. I believe building a romantic relationship on an already established friendship can be a very good idea. What *would* destroy the friendship is immorality and guilt. If the relationship is moral, the friendship does not have to disappear when the romantic commitment breaks down. The friendship may change in terms of openness and the amount of time spent together, but it does not have to leave behind resentment and bitterness.

Fourth, the break between the two young people who have developed an intimate sexual relationship is almost equivalent to a divorce between married partners. We know that divorce can produce great hurt, anger, a fear of future commitments, and a sense of bitterness. Young people are even more vulnerable than adults who divorce one another after years of commitment. The deep hurt they experience in breaking a sexually-involved relationship has in some cases led to depression and even suicide or homicide.

It makes sense to wait until marriage before engaging in genital sexuality, from an emotional and moral point of view. It also makes sense to wait in terms of having respect for the life that could be conceived as a result of sexual intercourse. It is only through a commitment to a lifelong sexual love relationship that the necessary stability can exist to bring children into this world. I must emphasize that people do not simply become spouses when they get married, they are opening themselves to parenthood. A sexual relationship is an expression of deep, intimate love; it is also the way to procreate. Life and sexuality are enmeshed.

What is the best preparation for responsible, life-giving sexual behavior in adulthood? The best preparation is years of training in regulating sexuality through the virtue of chastity. Instead, some adults and adolescents wrongly claim that sexual experimentation is good for teens and young adults. They argue it gives them an opportunity to practice the physical aspects of sex and get their sexual desires out of their systems so they can later be faithful to their spouses and avoid having mid-life crises. Not so! You are not supposed to get sexual desire out of your system. Rather, sexual desire persists and even increases. You will need to regulate and control it throughout your entire life.

Actually, sexual involvement with different partners during the teenage years, in addition to confusing our understanding and appreciation of love, can make us *more* vulnerable to sexual infidelity later in life. Temptations to engage in extramarital relations are abundant in adult life. These worldly allurements to be unfaithful can be accentuated in the lives of those who have grown accustomed to multiple sexual partners during their teenage and young adult years. Chastity must be practiced by Christians, even within marriage, and the best preparation for a faithful love commitment in the future is to practice the virtue of chastity from one's youth.

"Safe sex" is a popular term these days, but this label is actually anti-life. The main idea behind it is to provide unmarried couples with a variety of ways to have sexual relations while minimizing their fear of pregnancy. People mainly promote this anti-life attitude through contraceptives, which I will discuss in Chapter 14. Safe sex is also promoted as a way to reduce the possibility of acquiring sexually transmitted diseases (STDs) like AIDS as a result of having had sexual intercourse with an infected person. (Chapter 15 covers these diseases.) Society today appears to be preoccupied with health concerns and population control, while it ignores the more complex responsibilities of life, love, and the moral order.

Life and love cannot be pulled apart as the ultimate ends of human sexuality, which must be understood within the context of a moral order. Even if the risk of creating a new life or acquiring a disease could be totally avoided, the risk of serious emotional hurt would still be present. In addition, protecting these two very important elements of life and love within the marriage commitment preserves the moral order of our society.

The only logical, proven way to handle these crucial issues of life and love is to abstain from genital sex before marriage by practicing the virtue of chastity. Some adults think that teaching abstinence to impulsive teenagers is a useless endeavor. I believe that is an unfair assessment of young people offered by adults who have perhaps not given the best example through their own behavior. Teens understand well that waiting until marriage before having genital sex is the best and safest solution to today's sexual problems. They need *support* in their efforts to live healthy and moral lifestyles, not discouragement from disillusioned adults.

The "**chastity solution**" enhances love, protects life and strengthens the moral order in our society. The Church reaffirms Christian belief in the value of the permanent family unit when it preaches that genital sexuality must be practiced exclusively within the context of marriage. In fact, all major religions believe in the sacredness of the marriage commitment that men and women make to each other in order to create life and support one another and their offspring throughout their lives.

13

Homosexuality

Some young people are clearly aware of their sexual attraction to people of the opposite sex at an early stage in their lives. This sexual interest of a man in a woman or a woman in a man is called **heterosexuality**. Other young people experience no particular interest in sexual matters until they are a little older. They cannot define any particular sexual interests, and their attention is directed toward their family, school, hobbies, sports, or other activities. Some children and adolescents experience some degree of heterosexuality and some sexual attraction toward people of their same gender. This sexual interest of one man in another man or one woman in another woman is called **homosexuality**.

Doubts about sexual identity are common during the years of sexual development, especially between ages ten and sixteen. Some doctors think that full sexual identity is not achieved until after the teenage years. In other words, some teens may experience a combination of heterosexual and homosexual interests, or **bisexuality**; some may report strong heterosexual or homosexual interests; some may report no particular sexual interest. Doubts about sexual identity should be brought out into the open and discussed with parents. Concerns about homosexuality should be shared with parents. It is always best to share our doubts, rather than to think something is wrong with our development. We should not agonize in secret about our sexual fears, whether these fears have to do with homosexuality or anything else.

Why, you may ask, do some kids experience more doubts than others? There is no clear answer, but here are some ideas. Every family is unique in its approach to sexuality and expressions of affection. Children are different in their perceptions of the world around them, their responses to that world, and their life experiences. Each interest, attraction, or experience may open the child up to sexual responses and sexual doubts.

- One child may be very attentive to his or her body and its reactions and feelings, and another may not care at all.
- One child may have been exposed to sexual materials or experiences early on, and another not at all. The reaction to that exposure is also unique and different.
- One child may have a positive sexual reaction to a childhood sexual experience, another may react with fear, and still another with repulsion.
- One child may have been sexually abused, while another was not. Even the responses to the abuse may be different for each child.

Different childhood sexual experiences can translate into differences in sexual development during puberty and early adolescence. You should not compare yourself with others. You are unique, growing up in a unique environment. As I have said before: "*To yourself be true.*" It is best to be honest about who you are today. Above all, you should avoid any thoughts that some other boy or girl is better or more normal than you are.

Questions or doubts about gender identity are best handled by asking parents for help, and by consulting a professional who can help clarify aspects of sexual development and facilitate emotional growth. This kind of consultation is particularly important for teens who are worried that they are not sufficiently interested in the opposite sex. An experienced Christian counselor can help a young person differentiate a homosexual attraction that entirely excludes any interest in members of the opposite sex from a need for a strong identification with his or her gender. I believe this identification involves a borrowing of masculinity or femininity in order to develop healthily. For example, it may mean that a boy admires the good looks, muscular development, or other physical or emotional characteristics of a man. A girl may feel attracted to the beauty, shape, or other characteristics of a woman. These attractions may at times produce sexual feelings. These feelings should be understood and regulated, but their presence is not an indication of homosexuality. Some authors call these feelings "pseudo (i.e., false) homosexuality" since their appearance is only a reminder of a normal stage in sexual development.

Some teens feel they do not fit with other people of their same age and sex. For example, boys who do not like sports at all or girls who are very interested in guys' sports may think they are abnormal. Our society sends these kinds of unhelpful hidden messages: boys must like sports (Be tough! Be a man!); girls must be "lady-like" (whatever that means!—society is very clear in the case of boys and far less so on girls' choices of hobbies and clothing). I should emphasize that not fitting into a certain pattern of gifts, talents, or interests does not exclude people from their own gender. Hobbies or interests are not primary aspects of being a man or a woman. Parents, try to be mindful to learn, respect, and support your children's natural talents and interests even when these things do not fit preconceived ideas of what they "should" be doing. Expose your children to different healthy activities, but don't force them against their will to engage in activities they are not interested in or suited to pursue.

Some teens feel mature beyond their age; others feel immature. Each teen develops emotionally at his or her own rate and that doesn't make them more or less masculine or feminine. All these personal interests or conflicts need to be addressed during adolescence. Parents, you need to be aware of these differences and able to discuss them constructively without pushing your children too far beyond their comfort zone. You should help your children stretch and grow in areas of social relations where they may be a bit shy or apprehensive. Children and teens usually can accept the challenge if given the proper amount of parental support. However, if the gentle push to grow turns into a fight and increased resistance, then both the parents and the child need to look at the situation carefully or seek assistance from a third party.

Some adult men and women, through no fault of their own, are exclusively homosexual. They only have sexual feelings for members of their own sex. Some doctors study the possibility of a genetic predisposition to homosexuality. Other doctors study the childhood experiences that could have led to a homosexual adjustment rather than a heterosexual one. No ultimate conclusions have been reached. Some men and women who have been engaged in homosexual relations report that through prayer and Christian counseling they have changed their sexual orientation. Other homosexuals disagree and do not think this type of change is possible for them. As I have said, young people should share their concerns with their parents in order to manage their sexual feelings effectively.

Every human being—independent of their sexual orientation—is God's unique creation, has the same dignity, and is loved by him and made for him. Homosexual persons must be treated with respect and given equal opportunities for progress and success in our society. Homosexual men and women can be excellent friends, and successful in every area of life. Sexual jokes and insults are offensive and must be avoided; these remarks are often the result of fears and ignorance about sexuality. People should be mature about these and other sexual matters and not engage in bashing and insults.

Men and women with a homosexual orientation should make every effort to understand their sexuality in order to live healthy and productive lives. They must challenge themselves to live dedicated Christian lives. They too are called to holiness, and they too are stewards of God's creation, responsible to make this world the best one possible. Their biggest challenge and sacrifice is to abstain from genital sexuality. Genital sex, it has been said, is reserved for those who enter into the sacrament of Matrimony. Genital sex should not be practiced outside this permanent commitment that is open to life and love. Both heterosexual and homosexual men and women must regulate their sexual impulses by practicing the virtue of chastity.

Take time to discuss homosexual doubts and fears with your parents. Discuss also the respect that those who have a homosexual orientation deserve.

14

Family Planning

The wife and the husband are the foundation of the family. Children come from their union. Parents are responsible not only to give their children life, but also to provide for their physical, emotional, educational, spiritual, and financial needs. The process that parents go through to decide in front of God their ability to have more children and provide adequately for them, is called **family planning**.

Only married couples need to be concerned with family planning. The best plan unmarried people can make is to plan not to engage in genital sex. Unmarried people who want to have sex also want to avoid the consequences of their actions. I have referred to this before as the "anti-life" mentality of our society. Married people do not want to avoid the responsibility of parenthood; on the contrary, they want to have children responsibly.

Married people can exert their responsibility in a natural or artificial way. **Natural Family Planning** (NFP) revolves around the female menstrual cycle, the woman's body temperature throughout the month, and other variables. The couple abstains from sexual intercourse during the days that the woman is fertile, during which sexual intercourse could result in a pregnancy. Nothing artificial is used and a bit of sacrifice is required, since the couple cannot have sex on certain days of the month. **Artificial birth control** involves the use of objects or medications that prevent the pregnancy. No method of birth control, natural or artificial, works perfectly. When a couple engages in the act of sexual love there is always a chance, big or small, that the act could result in a pregnancy—unless the woman is already pregnant, of course.

This book is not designed for married couples who have to discern their responsibility in front of God regarding their families' needs and their choice of family planning. There are very good books that cover that material well. Suffice it to say that the Catholic Church in particular is very challenging in this regard. It invites couples to recognize the value of small and big sacrifices, both in having a family and in regulating the birth of their children only through natural methods.

Rather, this book is designed to help younger teens develop as sexually responsible persons. Teens should not be concerned with specific methods of birth control because they should not engage in genital sex before they are married. Young people, if they are curious or concerned, should always check with their parents before contacting any counselor, clinic, or organization to learn more about contraception. Parents need to advise teens on the values and principles of people and organizations that offer family planning information. I always recommend seeking advice from counselors who have a faith-filled, Christian viewpoint.

The media delivers a lot of information about **contraceptives**, another name for artificial birth control methods. I believe they emphasize the use of contraceptives because they think teens will not wait to have sex until they are married, and that contraceptives constitute a lesser evil than unwanted pregnancies. I disagree with those who have given up on teens and think they are too impulsive and unable to control their sexual desires. I say they are wrong: young people *can* understand the facts and strengthen themselves to wait until marriage before having genital sex.

The fact remains that young people are curious about artificial birth control because popular culture is saturated with information about—and advertisements for—various contraceptive methods. To provide proper knowledge and understanding, I will mention two of these methods: condoms and the birth control pill. These and other methods have different degrees of effectiveness, and carry with them the possibility of adverse medical complications. In addition, contraceptives contribute to an anti-life mentality, and an erroneous, easy way out of responsible sexual behavior.

Much has been said about **condoms**. Condoms are used by men. A condom is like the finger of a plastic glove that fits over the penis. Semen gathers at the tip of the condom and is disposed of after the sexual act is finished. Condoms are not as safe as some teens think: there is still a one-in-ten chance of conceiving a child when the man uses a condom. Condoms became popular years ago because some thought they would help prevent sexually transmitted diseases. The fact is that condoms are even less effective in preventing the transmission of diseases than they are in preventing pregnancy.

Much also has been publicized about the **birth control pill**. It is used by women to prevent either the release of the egg cell from the ovary, or the implantation of a fertilized egg in the uterus. If the egg is not implanted, the newly conceived human being is killed. In those cases, the pill is abortive (i.e., it produces an abortion). Although statistically it has a smaller margin of error regarding pregnancy prevention than other contraceptives, it can have serious medical complications. Also, if the woman forgets to take it on a daily basis, it could actually *increase* her chances of getting pregnant.

In addition to all the arguments in favor of pre-marital chastity and against the use of artificial birth control, there is one more piece of practical advice I would like to offer. A woman should not be too eager to trust a man who carries condoms around just in case they are needed. The condoms' availability should give her the opportunity to reflect on the man's motives and values. Similarly, a man should be wary of the motives of a woman who uses birth control pills on a regular basis.

15

Sexually Transmitted Diseases

Sexually transmitted diseases (STDs) are illnesses contracted through genital sex with a person who has the disease. They may also be transmitted through direct contact with blood from an infected person. You may also hear them called "VD," for venereal disease, which was their common name some years ago. STDs are viruses or bacteria—germs that can be found in sexual fluids and in the blood. There are many different sexually transmitted diseases but those most commonly mentioned are **human immunodeficiency virus** (HIV, which leads to **AIDS**), **gonorrhea**, **chlamydia**, **syphilis**, and **herpes**.

If a person has had sexual intercourse and in the next week or two finds a sore or pimple on the genitals, or experiences genital redness, swelling, pain, or a burning sensation, he or she should contact a physician and get tested. HIV is particularly difficult to detect, and women sometimes take longer to exhibit the symptoms of any sexual disease. Anyone who has sex outside marriage should get tested. If discovered early, gonorrhea, chlamydia and syphilis can be cured with antibiotics. Herpes cannot be cured but can be managed with medication. AIDS is an incurable disease at present, but it can be treated to extend the span and quality of life of the infected person when it is detected early.

Since AIDS is incurable and of epidemic proportions, it has set our society into a panic. Overwhelmed by this tragic illness, some people blame God for its occurrence, and others consider it a punishment from God. Neither position is acceptable when you think of a loving and caring God. The human body is fragile and at some point dies and returns to God, whether the illness that killed it is sexually transmitted or not. AIDS is neither God's fault nor God's punishment. We must pray fervently for a cure to this disease and challenge scientists to continue looking for a cure and a vaccine to prevent it from happening. We must be helpful in caring for AIDS victims and their families rather than rejecting them or being judgmental.

The public is very concerned about HIV and other STDs. We feel helpless and out of control when we are confronted with illnesses we do not fully understand and cannot cure. It is with this perception of powerlessness that some people advocate what they call "safe sex"—a set of practices that I call neither safe nor moral. It is in this context that the use of condoms has increased, making teens believe they are not risking illness, and indirectly teaching that sex outside marriage is acceptable. Although many of these people mean well, I believe they confuse teens and young adults. Please remember that physical, emotional, and moral safety is achieved exclusively through abstinence supported by the virtue of chastity.

If two people love each other and one of them is ill and contagious (i.e., the other person can catch the disease) I believe the most loving action would be to make sure the loved one does not catch the illness. It is difficult to understand why someone who is HIV positive would have sex with a person they love, thereby risking that person's health and life. I find no reason for such action except a personal need for sexual pleasure. Sacrificial love should surpass the desire for pleasure. Even if the loved one insisted on their willingness to risk catching the disease, it appears irresponsible to engage in the sexual act.

Sometimes teens worry about STDs more than they should. Teens who choose not to be involved in genital sex outside marriage and are not sharing dirty needles as a result of drug addiction will not have to face any of these diseases. However, if teens who have not had sexual contact, still experience a rash, redness, pain, or any other symptoms in the genital area, they should still consult a doctor. There are other illnesses besides the sexually transmitted ones that require medical treatment.

16

Other Sexual Issues

Popular culture, especially in the pornographic media, tends to emphasize ignoble aspects of sexuality. It confuses young people with distorted ideas about sexuality, graphic representations of perverted acts, and sexual paraphernalia. I detest having to pay attention to these issues, because they negatively affect our thinking and our healthy sexual development. At the same time, it is to protect and promote this healthy development that I must raise and discuss them.

I have to state my disappointment with irresponsible adults who desecrate sexuality with what they print, make, and joke about, forcing me to comment on these issues. Under the contention that such adults are free to choose whatever they want, and under the protection of the "freedom of speech," they induce sexual addictions. In addition, they make money from the curious and the addicted, they confuse people, and they attempt to destroy God's beautiful gift of sexuality.

So-called adult pornographic stores sell *sexual paraphernalia*, the media advertises it, and the subject comes up in TV programs. As a result, some young people end up nervously joking or wondering about such things as inflatable dolls with which to practice sex, artificial penises called "dildos," vibrators used to stimulate the genital area, and perfumes that supposedly enhance the sexual experience. All of these items are against Christian values. If we reflect a bit, we quickly realize that none of these objects enhance the principles of love and life. On the contrary, inflatable dolls and dildos would most likely be used for masturbation, which in itself is disordered. In addition, a loving couple does not need vibrators or toys in order to enjoy their act of love. If a married couple is experiencing difficulties, it is questionable that these objects would resolve their problems and help them appreciate their mutual love. The best advice is to stay clear of pornographic stores and objects.

Sperm banks and *artificial insemination* have also been widely discussed in the media and young people ask about them all the time. I will describe them in reference to horses. Semen can be obtained from a male horse, then frozen and saved in a sperm bank. The semen can then be given or sold to a breeder who has a female horse. The semen is inserted into the female horse through the process called artificial insemination. The two horses never have sex directly but the sperm cells, inserted in the female horse at the right time within the menstrual cycle, may end up in a pregnancy. Maybe this is okay when it comes to horses, but for humans? It lends itself to all kinds of abuses: genetic selection according to intelligence or race, a sexuality devoid of love and commitment between the parents, the purposeful absence of the father, and others.

Oral and anal sex are widely depicted and talked about in the pornographic media. Oral sex involves physical contact between the genitals of one person and the mouth of the other. There has been such propaganda about oral sex that some young people could be led to believe it is better than sexual intercourse, which is not true. It is important to realize that it is acceptable *not* to want to engage in oral sex. On the other hand, if two spouses are united in marriage, they can engage in touching any part of the other spouse's body with any part of their own body, if they both agree, during sexual love. It is important to note that although the two bodies are one as a result of marriage, spouses must treat each other with respect, and appreciate the particular wishes and desires of the other spouse. In any case, it should be obvious that the sexual act is to reach its climax open to life and love, with the semen deposited inside the vagina and nowhere else.

Concerning anal sex, most medical authorities, whether Christian or not, warn against it. The large intestine and the anus are the organs that release the body's solid waste or feces. The anus is designed to push out the feces, not to have objects inserted in it. Inside the anus there are hemorrhoid vessels that can be hurt by forcing something inside it. No matter how clean, the anus still has remnants of feces inside it. It is difficult to understand why the pornographic media wants to emphasize anal sex as good and pleasurable. Perhaps they are running out of "new" ideas and they have to come out with very obviously unattractive and medically unsound ideas. Perhaps they are encouraging forms of sexual expressions that are in line with the "anti-life" attitude of those who promote a deviant sexuality that avoids pregnancy. Keep in mind that deviant sex is more closely related to expressions of power and domination than to expressions of care and mutual love. Also keep in mind that deviant sex does not prevent sexually transmitted diseases, and often increases the chances of contracting an illness.

In addition, there are sexual disorders related to serious emotional problems. One such disorder is *rape*. Rape involves an act of sexual intercourse forced on the victim through seduction, intimidation, or violence. It is usually an attack by a man upon a woman. It is called "date rape" when it involves seduction on the part of someone the victim knows. In this case, the sex act is still forced on the victim, who has not consented to it. When this happens, the victim should immediately go to a hospital emergency room and seek medical help. Victims of rape or other forms of sexual abuse should also seek psychological help. Counseling is helpful because victims often experience depression, guilt, anger, and other emotions that need to be dealt with in order to help them regain their emotional and sexual health.

There are other major sexual disorders. *Pedophilia* is the sexual abuse of a child by an adult, a topic I covered at the end of Chapter 9. *Voyeurism* involves sexual pleasure from looking at the sexual parts or watching the sexual acts of other people. It is also called being a "peeping Tom" when it involves the habit of spying on people as they are getting undressed. *Exhibitionism* is the public exposure of one's genitals by an adult. *Bestiality* is sexual involvement with an animal. *Transvestism* is cross-dressing (i.e., dressing in clothes designed for the opposite sex and acting accordingly). *Transsexualism* is a compulsive desire to actually become a member of the opposite sex.

Prostitution is having sexual relations for money. It may be a sexual disorder in some cases but it is certainly a social disorder in all cases. Ignorance, poverty, and drug use have accompanied this problem through the centuries. Prostitution is illegal in most countries and has usually involved women. There are also male prostitutes whose sex customers are usually homosexual. Young runaways often engage in prostitution as a result of financial needs, and end up getting a sexually transmitted disease or being abused by those who run the business. Prostitutes should seek help so they can look at their problems and find other means of financial support.

If a person repeatedly engages in fantasies or behaviors that are sexually disordered, he or she should seek help. These disorders are very serious, and in some cases, such as in rape, pedophilia, being a "peeping Tom," exhibitionism, and prostitution, they are considered illegal. People with these disorders are themselves victims of their often uncontrollable sexual problems. They should receive help, and we should pray for their recovery. At the same time, society has an obligation to protect people from them.

Young people who are going through puberty and adolescence sometimes experience a sexual reaction when they hear or think about these sexual problems. They need to recognize their feelings, but they do not need to panic about them. These reactions may be related to insecurities, a need for power, or an overall sense of nervousness regarding sex. However, it is best to discuss these doubts and reactions with a parent, counselor, or another trusted adult whenever the sexual feelings are confusing or produce unnecessary anxiety.

We are now facing as a society a number of complicated issues regarding reproductive technology. Scientific experiments related to test-tube babies, surrogate parenting, cloning, and the production of babies outside the womb, involve very complex moral issues. While scientific research should continue to advance, the morality of specific studies and conclusions should not be ignored. All these issues involve very complicated ethical and moral issues, and dealing with them would require another, more complicated book.

The most important principle to remember remains constant: God has created us out of love, and made us capable of transmitting life. Life and love should be expressed through genital sex, exclusively within the sacrament of Matrimony, between spouses who share a lifelong commitment to love one another and the children they bring into this world.

17

Called to Holiness

Sexual doubts and insecurities can be obstacles to one's growth as a healthy and holy person. The purpose of this book has been to provide appropriate information in a very significant area of our lives. It is through adequate knowledge, and open discussion with parents and other trusted adults, that you can best regulate your sexual impulses and desires. However, no one book can answer all questions or resolve all doubts, and we must always keep on asking and sharing our ideas.

The information in this book will hopefully help you form an adequate moral conscience and strengthen your determination to be chaste. Ultimately, happiness is the goal of all human beings, and it cannot be achieved without love. True love must be based on commitment and personal sacrifice for the loved one. Chastity is the virtue that protects our love relations, helps us to integrate our sexual desires and moral values, and strengthens us to live up to our commitments. Jesus' teaching is both challenging and reassuring:

> As the Father loves me, so I also love you. Remain in my love. If you keep my commandments, you will remain in my love, just as I have kept my Father's commandments and remain in His love. (Jn 15: 9-10)

We are loved by Christ, just as he and the Father love one another. Love must underlie all human relationships and be based on God's commandments. The fourth commandment—"honor your father and your mother"—reminds us of the importance of the family as the place where life and love find their human origins. In its English translation, the sixth commandment—"you shall not commit adultery"—seems to apply only to married people. But in other languages it translates as "you shall not fornicate," a broader instruction that refers to all genital sexual activity outside of marriages that are committed to life and love. The ninth commandment—"you shall not covet your neighbor's wife"—reminds us that sins of the flesh begin in one's mind and heart, and that we are responsible for what we consent to think about. Together, these three commandments protect human love. To keep these commandments, we must practice the virtue of chastity. And Jesus goes on:

> I have told you this so that my joy may be yours and your joy may be complete. This is my commandment: love one another as I have loved you. There is no greater love than this: to lay down one's life for one's friends. (Jn 15:11-13)

Keeping the commandments brings us joy; agreeing to love others as Christ loves us brings us complete joy. Christ loved us to the end and laid down his life for us. Christian love demands commitment and sacrifice from us in order to care for those we love. It challenges us to always place the needs of the loved one ahead of our own. It implies we should always keep in mind what is best for the person we claim to love. It means we are willing to die for that person. If genital sexual behavior is to deserve the title of "sexual love," it should only be expressed when these characteristics of commitment and sacrifice are present.

God made us out of love, free to love the One who is the Source of All Love. This intimate relationship with the one who made us makes us holy. We are called to holiness. We should treat those around us with love, aware that they too belong to God. Prepare yourself for tomorrow's big commitments through today's small sacrifices made out of love for God and others.

Thank you for reading this book. Please keep it and review it as often as necessary. And may the Lord transform the world into a most loving place through our common desire for goodness and holiness.

Notes